Robert Eagle

Alternative
Medicine

Futura Publications Limited
A Futura Book

A Futura Book

First published in Great Britain by
Futura Publications Limited in 1978

Copyright © Robert Eagle 1978

Extract from *The Pain Game* by C. Norman Shealy, M.D.

Reprinted by permission of Celestial Arts,
Millbrae, California, U.S.A.

Copyright © 1976 by C. Norman Shealy.

To Catharine
And with thanks to the many people who helped me
in my research, especially those who were rash
enough to let me quote them.

ISBN 0 7088 1464 6

Printed by
William Collins Sons & Co. Ltd
Glasgow

Futura Publications Limited
110 Warner Road, Camberwell
London SE5

Robert Eagle was born in 1948 and educated at Gresham's School and Magdalene College, Cambridge. He was a staff writer with the *General Practitioner* magazine from 1974 to 1976, but from 1976 he has been a freelance journalist and broadcaster, contributing to BBC radio, *The Sunday Times*, The *Observer*, *World Medicine*, *General Practitioner*, *Books and Bookmen* and many others. Robert Eagle is the Editor of *Pain Topics* medical magazine.

Contents

Introduction—The Medical Underground

Twenty thousand people in Britain today are practising medicine without any official qualification or approval. About a quarter of them make a full-time living from their various therapies, even though the majority would be regarded as quacks even by the organizations which have been set up to promote unorthodox forms of medicine.

Patients who are tempted to seek the help of these practitioners have hardly any means of establishing whether their therapies are genuine, dangerous or useless. The literature provided by many of the associations which represent particular styles of alternative medicine contains many impressive claims which have not been subjected to the rigours of scientific trial. This aggravates doctors, but it does not harm the unorthodox practitioners, whose business is booming as never before.

At the same time apparently sane and sensible doctors are showing discontent with mainstream medicine and are exploring these alternatives for themselves, even though in the terms of most contemporary scientific thinking they are apparently unworkable and beneath contempt.

Until very recently a doctor who consorted professionally with an unqualified practitioner was liable to be struck off the medical register. A doctor who flirted with the unorthodox therefore had to be bold or foolhardy, or have indulgent colleagues. The uneasiness bred by this situation led to the formation of at least one secret medical organization which encouraged its members to pursue their unorthodox interests but also protected their identities from the unsympathetic.

Before you read any further I had better warn you that almost no mention will be made in this book of colour therapy,

7

magnetism, orgone, aroma therapy, zone therapy, iris diagnosis, alchemy, rolfing, Pyonex treatment, Niehans cell therapy, Exaltation of Flowers, Bach remedies, hand diagnosis, mega-vitamins, African witch doctors, Unani-Tibi, let alone the self-help techniques of Hatha Yogi, T'ai Chi, macrobiosis and the Alexander Method.

If you want to know more about them than their myriad colourful names you will have to seek elsewhere. I am assured that they all work wonders.

The aim of this book is twofold: first, to give an idea of how some doctors and lay practitioners have sought to explain medical phenomena which *they* know to be real but which do not fit with orthodox thinking; second, to point out that 'natural' medicine, 'alternative' medicine, 'fringe' medicine, 'future' medicine – call it what you will – is not necessarily safe medicine. If Nature were safe, we would not fall ill in the first place. During my researches I picked up a pamphlet in the thriving herbal clinic. It read thus:

NO DRUGS – NO SIDE EFFECTS – THE SAFE ALTERNATIVE

In an age of pollution, chemicalization of foodstuffs, artificial flavouring and colouring, it is good to get back to NATURE. That which is NATURE IS SAFE, that which is NATURAL IS SENSIBLE and that which is NATURAL IS WITHOUT THE DANGEROUS SIDE-EFFECTS of modern drugs which are so alarming today. So many people are suffering from iatro-genic (drug-caused) disease, let alone their original con-dition.

THE SAFE AND EFFECTIVE ALTERNATIVE IS HERBAL MEDICINE

What it does not mention is that parsley can cause haemorr-hage, sage can induce an abortion, and thyme, if you are not too careful where you pick it, can give you lead poisoning.

And take this snippet from the *Register and Yearbook of the Acupuncture Association:*

In fact, nowadays the series of diseases which claim most victims are caused by drugs used to treat other illnesses.

8

Acupuncture, on the other hand, has no side-effects; it is not addictive; and when it does not work, rarely, when used correctly, does harm.

It was sensible of that author to add the phrase 'when used correctly'. Otherwise one might wonder what caused the hepatitis which has already afflicted a number of British acupuncturists' patients or, indeed, the collapsed lung which brought about the untimely demise of a Scandinavian patient undergoing acupuncture.

'No side-effects' has become a rallying cry for practitioners of unorthodox medicine. It is, unfortunately, nonsense. Even healing by laying-on-of-hands has side-effects, though, as we shall see, they tend to affect the healer rather than the patient.

Orthodox medicine is widely known to have side-effects because we can read about them in the paper every day. It took thalidomide to make us really scared about drugs and their side-effects. Until then millions had been happily making their stomachs bleed by swallowing daily handfuls of aspirin. Just after antibiotics had been discovered in the Second World War, troops gobbled vast quantities of the new medicine to protect themselves from getting VD, little knowing that they were helping to breed resistant bacteria. Since then we have had diethylstilboestrol (a hormone given to women to prevent spontaneous abortion, subsequently found to cause vaginal cancer in some of their girl children), the MAO inhibitors (antidepressant drugs which can cause brain haemorrhage if taken with certain foods), practolol (a heart drug which caused gut and eye disease), and whooping cough vaccine, which gave a few children irreparable brain damage. Aplastic anaemia, an extremely dangerous disorder of bone marrow, was once extremely rare. It became rather more common after the introduction of the anti-inflammatory drug, phenylbutazone. The Committee on the Safety of Medicines, which was set up in the wake of the thalidomide scandal, dispatched thirteen urgent warnings to doctors during its first twelve years telling them about hitherto unsuspected dangers of prescribed medicines.

Estimates vary, but it is thought that iatrogenic diseases, i.e. diseases caused by doctors or drugs, account for the presence of more than one in eight patients in hospital. In the United States the figure has been put at 30 per cent in some states.

In 1967 two Canadian doctors, R. I. Ogilvie and J. Ruedy, reported that in a survey they had made of over 700 hospital patients in a general medical unit, 26.4 per cent suffered from adverse consequences of drug therapy. In 1976 Dr Eamonn Fottrell, a consultant at Tooting Bec hospital in London, took a random sample of 200 patients in long-stay psychiatric wards and found that half of them had been receiving unnecessary or excessive medication. When Dr P. F. D'Arcy, the professor of pharmacy at Queen's University, Belfast, reviewed over forty recent medical papers by doctors on both sides of the Atlantic dealing with adverse drug reactions, he felt moved to tell the Royal Society of Medicine that:

It has been conservatively estimated that 300,000 people require hospital treatment in the United States as a result of drug reaction; this makes iatrogenic disease one of the ten leading causes of hospitalization. Unfortunately the hazards do not end there, since once the patient is inside a hospital, the danger of an iatrogenic disease remains a threat to health or life, from the prescriptions written in the hospital. Multiple drug therapy and the resulting drug-interactions are the root cause of much of this problem.

The problem is that more than half the 2500 drugs which are now available for doctors to prescribe have been introduced relatively recently. Unless a doctor has taken care to brush up his knowledge of the new medicines marketed since he was a student, he may remain blithely unaware of their possible dangers. In 1975 medical researchers at the University of Aberdeen sent out a questionnaire to over 250 general practitioners working in north-east Scotland. The doctors were asked to say what they knew about the potential inter-actions of five types of commonly prescribed drugs. Their replies revealed that, on average, they had heard of only 17 per cent of the known interactions between those drugs. Almost all the doctors who returned the questionnaire asked to be given more information – information which was apparently not available to them from the medical literature they usually read.

Confusion about drugs is not confined to doctors. In September 1977 the regional pharmacist for the North-West Thames health authority, Dr P. Noyce, told the British Pharmaceutical Conference that:

> Many people forgot or deliberately omitted to take prescribed medicines. A survey showed that nearly half the patients used suppositories without removing the wrappers. Many people breathed out instead of in when using inhalers.

Surgery probably has almost as bad a record as drugs, though statistics are not so readily available. Surgeons at one of Britain's leading orthopaedic hospitals have told me that at least one in five of the laminectomy operations they perform to relieve back pain result in the patients suffering more pain than they did before. In the United States Dr Henry Simmons, a former senior official of the Department of Health, Education and Welfare, told me that large surveys made in hospitals had shown that 50 per cent of post-operative complications and 35 per cent of surgical deaths were preventable.

> After 30 years of performing radical breast surgery, we have only just begun to conduct trials to determine when it should be done. It has been found that many of these operations are unnecessary.

Dr Simmons is well qualified to comment on such matters. The US Government gave him the task of setting up a national scheme (Professional Standards Review Organizations) which would try to ensure that hospital patients received the treatment they actually required.

Discontent with the failures of modern medicine has prompted Ivan Illich, author of *Medical Nemesis*, to declare that 'the medical establishment has become a major threat to health'. Illich's message has not been scorned by all doctors; in 1976 Professor Thomas McKeown of Birmingham University in his book *The Role of Medicine: Dream, Mirage or Nemesis?* argued that 'medical intervention has made and can be expected to make a relatively small contribution to the prevention of sickness and death'.

This book is not intended to offer a critique of modern medicine. Others have done that very well already. Nor is it intended to suggest that we should reject drug medicine and surgery in favour of herbalism and psychic healing. Modern orthodox medicine has been subjected to an intense scrutiny and it has not fared particularly well under this examination. Unorthodox medicine has not undergone such scrutiny, and there is no reason to suppose that it would fare any better.

Sir Derrick Dunlop, the first chairman of the Committee on the Safety of Drugs, once said: 'Show me a medicine which has not got adverse effects, and I will show you a useless medicine.' Medicine, like witchcraft, can cure and it can kill. Its effects depend on the integrity, knowledge and competence of the practitioner.

What this book is intended to offer is an idea of what makes certain medical practices *orthodox* and others *unorthodox*. Most of the doctors whose work is described began as thoroughly orthodox practitioners. Most of them would in fact resent the implication that they are now unorthodox. They have lost none of their integrity and honesty by opting for heterodox pursuits. They still aim to understand and heal patients. Nevertheless, their ideas challenge the basis of conventional thinking and require a completely new philosophy before they can be understood and valued by the majority.

In the 1840s Dr James Esdaile, a surgeon working in India, reported that he had successfully performed over a thousand operations on hypnotized patients. The death rate, he claimed, was only six per cent. This was at a period when there were no antiseptics and a third of surgical patients in Britain died under the knife or from post-operative complications. Esdaile was howled down as a fraud, and his critics declared that he had bribed his patients to pretend they were not suffering.

One of his attackers suggested that, 'it was because they were hardened impostors that they let their legs be cut off and large tumours be cut out without showing any sign even of discomfort'.

How things have changed. A hundred and twenty years later acupuncturists who claimed that they were able to render patients pain-free with needles were told they were practising that well-known anaesthetic technique, hypnosis.

Professor Ian Stevenson, whose research into reincarnation phenomena is described in Chapter Eleven, tells a story of a Dutchman living in the East Indies, who tried to explain to a native how different Holland's climate was from that of Java. He said that in winter the water became so hard that you could walk on it. This notion struck the native as so absurd that he burst out laughing and would listen no more to the Dutchman's rantings. When Galileo found that the Earth moved round the Sun, his contemporaries refused to look through his telescope themselves lest their ideas on the nature of the Universe were upset.

Many of the therapies in this book have not been subjected to the kind of analysis which would convince a hard-headed scientist that they really worked. The main reason for this is that few have bothered to investigate them because they do not fit in with their idea of the Universe.

The popular idea of disease is that it is caused by bugs or chemicals invading the body from without. The body is thought to be a complex chemical structure, whose workings can be manipulated by the addition or subtraction of chemical substances. If you are attacked by a bug, you use an antibiotic to attack it. If a disease is seen to be associated with the deficit or excessive production of a chemical substance, the drug companies synthesize a chemical substance to set the problem right. And it works. It may cause a few other problems elsewhere in the body, but it does the specific job for which it was intended.

If you get spots on your tonsils, the answer is simple. Cut out your tonsils. It does not stop the bugs coming in, but they certainly can't land on your tonsils any more.

This materialist conception has no room for the idea of mind or consciousness. Brain, sure, you can see that and measure it. But mind, imagination, *soul*. Oh dear, oh dear. The mind, for those who still hankered after such notions, became regarded as something apart. There was you, and there was your body – and ne'er the twain shall meet.

The materialist philosophy still holds sway, though it seems to have been contradicted by modern physics. When we believed that everything was built from atoms, tiny indivisible bits of solid matter, materialism was a sensible philosophy. Those tiny bits of matter were the building blocks of the Universe.

Modern physics has shown not only that atoms are not the smallest units, but also that they are perhaps not matter at all. The particles which make up atoms are conceived of as energy. They are not little lumps of stuff, but dynamic processes. What we see as matter is a vast interconnection, a web of energy.

Einstein taught us that our way of observing space as three-dimensional was wrong. He added the fourth dimension of time. In his Theory of Relativity he pointed out that if the speed of light was constant, someone who observed an object closely would see it before another observer further away. An inhabitant of some distant star fifty light years away who turns his telescope towards earth will see what our parents saw fifty years ago. For day-to-day life three dimensions serve us very well because light moves so fast that, to all intents and purposes, we all perceive an event simultaneously. As soon as we introduce time into our method of observation, matter becomes elastic. A particle may appear solid if we freeze it in three dimensions; if we add time we recognize it as a process. Its mass turns into energy.

Particles are not like bricks, as atoms were once thought to be. In his book *The Tao of Physics* Dr Fritjof Capra, a researcher in theoretical high energy physics, says:

When two particles collide with high energies, they generally break into pieces, but these pieces are not smaller than the original particles. They are again particles of the same kind and are created out of the energy of motion involved in the collision process . . . The only way to divide subatomic particles further is to bang them together in collision processes involving high energies. This way we can divide matter again and again, but we never obtain smaller pieces because we just create particles out of the energy involved in the process. The subatomic particles are thus destructible and indestructible at the same time.

All this leave us wondering just what the material world is. Dr Capra's book points out that there are strong similarities between modern high energy physics and the ancient Oriental philosophies, which hold that there is no difference between mind and matter, that both are involved in external flux.

In 1930 Sir James Jeans FRS suggested that:

Today there is a measure of agreement, which on the physical side of science approaches almost to unanimity, that the stream of knowledge is heading towards a non-mechanical reality. The University begins to look more like a great *thought* than like a machine. Mind no longer appears as an accidental intruder into realms of matter.

Such thinking has inspired a few medics and scientists to investigate phenomena which were previously deemed ridiculous and/or fraudulent. In 1972 a group of them formed what must have been the most secretive medical and scientific association in Britain. Until 1977, when it held its first public meeting in London, the Scientific and Medical Network – known to its members as SMN or The Network – had kept a very low profile.

Only a handful of its 150 members allowed their affiliation to be known, and the identity of the rest was kept strictly confidential. Indeed a dozen of its members were so unwilling to disclose their interest in the Network that their names were known only to the association's two secretaries.

But in spite of all the trappings of a clandestine, revolutionary movement, nothing could be less threatening to civilized society than the Network. Its aims are spiritual rather than material, scientific rather than mercenary. The reason its members do not shout their beliefs from the roof tops is that they are afraid of being laughed at, scorned or even persecuted by their professional colleagues.

This gulf between the 'orthodox' and the 'unorthodox' makes Network doctors fearful of proclaiming their allegiance publicly. All the members I contacted agreed that the rule of confidentiality was adopted to protect them from jeopardizing their careers. 'If you are still on your way to a university chair, you are going to be a lot more cagey about professing unusual beliefs than if you have already got your chair,' the Network's medical secretary, Dr Patrick Shackleton, suggested.

The same holds true for other scientists; the scientific secretary, George Blaker, a former head of department at the Department of Education and Science, added:

> Orthodox colleagues would take a lesser view of your work if it was known that you were interested in fringe things. I suppose you cannot blame them for being suspicious of young men who are engaged in activities which could be judged unscientific.

But it is not just the young men whose identity is protected by the Network secretaries. Other members include a Nobel prize-winner, several fellows of the Royal Society and about fifty GPs and consultants, as well as another hundred scientists, economists, psychologists and philosophers.

Dr Shackleton, who later died in 1977, had been a consultant anaesthetist. He evinced little reluctance to talk about his role in the Network. He was primarily involved in recruiting academics into the association so that its philosophy would percolate through to more students. But Mr Blaker, displaying all the reserve one might expect of a senior civil servant, obviously thought it rather regrettable that a journalist should be writing about the Network at all. He stressed that the association had never sought publicity and membership was by invitation. A small number of eminent members do allow their names to be mentioned to convince prospective recruits of the association's respectability. Such names include former top government scientist Sir Kelvin Spencer and Air-Marshal Sir Victor Goddard, ex-principal of the College of Aeronautics. The Nobel prize-winner is Professor Brian Josephson, the Cambridge physicist and adviser to Maharishi Mahesh Yogi. (Should you wonder why a guru needs a scientific adviser, I must refer you back a few pages to Dr Capra's comments on mysticism and modern physics. Physicists like Josephson are also intrigued by the paranormal abilities – such as levitation – allegedly displayed by some experienced meditators.)

Network doctors were keen to declare that they were not dabbling in the occult. Dr Harold Parkes, a GP in Ross-on-Wye, for instance, actually practises nothing more unorthodox than manipulation on his patients with bad backs. But ever since he entered general practice in 1948 he has been well aware that his patients were using healers and other local fringe practitioners.

> I was taught by a dermatologist at medical school that the best cure for warts was a wart charmer. Sadly there aren't many of them left, but they were able to achieve 90 per cent success compared to 55 per cent with conventional therapy. And I used to get patients who asked if it was all right to use goose grease for rheumatism: I told them, 'If it works, then for God's sake use it!'

More recently Dr Parkes has become increasingly convinced of the powers of spiritual healers and is now prepared to refer patients to a local healer. He believes that such tactics make his patients more open with him: 'Lots of patients who would once have gone only to healers now come to me. Normally they wouldn't dare tell the doctor they had been to anyone unorthodox. I am also prepared to talk about religion – and that can help some people through their problems.'

While he was happy to encourage healing privately, he was reluctant to make his approval too public: 'It takes a lot of guts to stand up and be counted. I just did not want my name bandied about with the unorthodox.'

The discreet style of the Network, which puts *bona fide* practitioners in touch with others with similar interests, prevents names being bandied about.

Norfolk GP Ian Pearce, who practises laying on of hands as well as conventional allopathic medicine and encourages his patients to try prayer and meditation, is also wary of unqualified unorthodox practioners:

It would be desirable to bring alternative medicine into the NHS, though it would not be practical to do it quickly. Unless alternative medicine could put its house in order and introduce some kind of registration, the quacks would have a field day. Only recently I came across someone calling himself an acupuncturist: it turned out that he had learnt all he knew from a correspondence course.

Like other Network members Dr Pearce does not like the technological path taken by modern medicine:

Pathology can be spiritual or emotional as well as physical. Merely to treat the physical is like treating toothache with codeine. It is effective at first and stops the pain, but is useless in the long term. I am sure that 75 per cent of disease is self-created, the end of a psychosomatic chain. Disease is the product of stress interfering with body energies. I am sure many people live in happy symbiosis with their cancers – until something awful happens in their life and the thing then becomes really malignant.

He has found that healing by laying on hands can reverse this process in a willing patient: 'It won't work if the patient is passive – and sadly one of the troubles with our NHS is that patients no longer regard themselves as responsible for their health.'

One of the Network's most outspoken members is Dr Alec Forbes, consultant physician in Plymouth. As chairman of The Healing Research Trust, a charity sponsoring investigation of paranormal methods of healing, he has called for NHS recognition of all alternative practitioners – not only osteopaths, chiropractors and acupuncturists, but herbalists, healers, naturopaths and radionic practitioners too – in return for a formal system of registration.

Dr Forbes is not just a theorist; he treats his NHS out-patients by homoeopathy, acupuncture and radionics as well as by conventional therapy. He claims that homoeopathic remedies are especially useful for skin conditions with a success rate slightly better than orthodox medicines. When I spoke to him he told me he had one patient in hospital being treated by radionics: 'He suffers from a complicated condition, and drug therapy would offer more problems than solution. So I am not doing anything at all, except let him stay in bed and see if he responds to radionic treatment.' (Radionics is a form of distant healing, by which the practitioner 'tunes in' to a patient on an electromagnetic wavelength as yet undiscovered by mainstream science; see Chapter Two).

Dr Forbes came into conflict with his hospital colleagues by suggesting that he should run a clinical trial of the flower remedy Vita Florum. The hospital was about to be visited by a medical delegation who were to judge whether it was a suitable place for would-be GPs to hold training posts, and Dr Forbes was assured that 'if anything outlandish was going on' the hospital would be rejected. His local medical committee also turned down a proposed trial of radionics, claiming it would be unethical. (Dr Forbes believes that the committee was wrong; as long as a doctor was in charge of the project, there was nothing ethically objectionable.)

If he were still a registrar with twenty years to go in the profession, he would keep his interests to himself. 'But I kept things under my hat for far too long. I am now on a full-time contract and not far from retirement – and, quite honestly, I am past worrying about what people say.'

The Network is a strange organization, not only in its aims but in its structure. Its members tend to be either very young, idealistic recruits from the universities and medical schools or getting on in years, having reached a high enough position in their profession not to be afraid of jeopardizing their careers. What it has lacked is representatives from what might be called the middle management of science and medicine, people in their thirties or forties who are on their way up. To be vigorous, an organization needs such people.

Really, of course, there should be no need for such an organization at all. Secret societies are jolly good fun, but their very secrecy only reinforces the prejudice that their aims are weird and subversive. Aspiring scientists have avoided the fringe, believing that it was peopled exclusively by lunatics. Although much weirdness is to be found there, there is a lot which deserves a bit more looking into.

1 Healing—A Handy Remedy

'Put your hand between my hands,' Dr Sharma told me.

He held his own hands about four inches apart, while I slipped my right hand between them. There was a gap of at least an inch and a half on either side of my hand. I immediately felt a warm, rippling sensation in my hand, rather like a pleasant form of mild electric shock.

'That,' said Dr Sharma, 'is the healing energy.'

Sensations of warmth, tingling and gentle oscillation are reported by almost everyone who has received hand healing. One expects to experience such sensations when one is stroked or touched by another hand, especially if that hand belongs to a lover. But when the charge comes from a stranger and crosses thin air, it comes as a bit of a surprise.

Dr Arthur Bailey, the medical dowser whose work is described in the chapter on radiesthesia, relates how he was preparing to manipulate his brother's back:

> I was holding my hands up flat half an inch away from his spine. But before I had touched him, he told me to 'stop pushing'. He couldn't see what I was doing and said he thought I was trying to push him forward. His wife and I burst out laughing.

Dr Alec Forbes's wife, Nora, was being treated by a healer for low back pain. When the healer put his hands on her back, she felt a wiggling movement in her spine. 'It was as if a little mouse was moving under my skin.'

There are reckoned to be between 10,000 and 20,000 lay healers operating in Britain. The term 'healer' is better than the more popular phrases 'faith healer' and 'spiritual healer'.

Not all healers have a religious faith, nor do they require their patients to have such faith. 'Spiritual' is a more accurate description, but it is often confused with 'spiritualist'. Admittedly, some healers are spiritualists who believe that their power comes from a discarnate spirit, but they are rare in Europe. The psychic surgeons of Brazil and the Philippines would call themselves spiritualist healers.

Nothing could be simpler than healing: the healer simply lays hands on the patient, who promptly gets better. Some healers use prayer and meditation and encourage their patients to do likewise. Others are distant healers, who find that the power of thought alone can help patients far away.

The most spectacular healing cures, which attract most publicity, tend to be of chronic conditions like cancer and arthritis. Tumours shrivel and disappear, and joints which have been locked for years are suddenly freed. Sceptical medics describe such cancer cures as spontaneous remission (though God only knows what that means), and point out that a painful, cramped joint can be caused by hysteria as well as by osteoarthritis.

Hysteria (and that's another woolly term used to describe poorly understood psychological phenomena) can cure as well as cripple. There is no shortage of well-documented cases of wheelchair-bound individuals leaping up at public meetings to announce that they can walk again. A week later they are back in the wheelchair, sadder and possibly wiser.

And there is much evidence of the sceptic's friend – good old-fashioned fraud. In his book *Occult Medicine Can Save Your Life*, Dr Norman Shealy cites two cases of healthy American women who were paid a regular fee by evangelists to hobble down the aisle of a meeting hall on crutches. Once they had been touched by the preacher man, they would throw their sticks into the air, crying 'I'm healed, I'm saved'.

Healing does of course have the most respectable antecedents in Western civilization. Jesus Christ was a healer who cured by the touch of a hand and by a number of more extraordinary methods such as rubbing spittle and clay into a blind man's eyes. Modern Christians who accept the truth of the Gospel miracles are often more reluctant to accept that mortals possess the same abilities. Some churchmen do keep up the healing ministry, but they are regarded as somewhat suspect by the Establishment.

When little Bernadette Soubirous saw the Virgin Mary in the caves at Lourdes in 1858, the Vatican was embarrassed rather than delighted. These days, of course, Lourdes is a great money spinner. In an attempt to ensure that healing at Lourdes did not become a dangerous cult, the Catholic Church laid down strict rules for deciding which cures were miraculous and which were not. To be regarded as a miracle a cure had to fulfil several criteria: the disease must have been medically diagnosed as serious and difficult to cure; it should not be liable to clear up suddenly by spontaneous remission; previous medical treatment should have failed; the cure should be sudden and complete; and there should be no relapse.

Less than a hundred cures reported by Lourdes pilgrims have been judged miraculous. Remarkable recoveries there may have been, but they have not fulfilled the criteria. Not long after the First World War, Jack Traynor, a soldier who had been grievously wounded at Gallipoli, was taken to Lourdes. Machine-gun bullets had ripped through the nerves of his right arm, which was paralysed as a result. He was paraplegic, doubly incontinent and had a hole in his skull left by one of the ten surgeons whose hands he had passed through. He was also epileptic. To his physicians' amazement he not only survived the journey but underwent an astounding recovery. The hole in his head healed, the epilepsy disappeared, he regained the use of his limbs – and took up work as a coal heaver. His cure was *not* adjudged miraculous, however. Apparently the medical panel decided that his paralysis could have been caused by hysteria, and the epilepsy – well, epilepsy comes and goes in strange ways, so that could have been a spontaneous remission.

Even so, in 1951 the British psychiatrist D. J. West surveyed the evidence presented for eleven cures which the Church's panel had passed as miracles. He reported that all of them were open to alternative explanation and suggested that

23

the Church and its medical advisers were overly gullible. (Dr West has been the scourge of investigators into the paranormal. As a young man he worked as research officer for the Society for Psychical Research but gave up the job because his experiments had consistently negative results. Other parapsychologists cite him as an example of the sceptical observer whose questioning mind disturbs psychic phenomena. Although he was attracted by the paranormal, he later concentrated his studies on homosexuality and criminology, two forms of abnormal psychology which were more amenable to the analytic approach.)

Dr Daniel O'Connell, a consultant radiotherapist at London's Charing Cross Hospital, has served on the international medical panel which decides whether cures at Lourdes are miraculous or not. He also accompanies a party of pilgrims to Lourdes every year. As a Catholic he is sceptical of hand healing though he is quite prepared to believe that cures can be miraculously brought about by God. Ninety per cent of healing is 'suggestion', he says, and does not reverse the the natural course of a disease. 'If you believe in the absolute power of God, you can believe in miracles. Miracles do reverse natural trends.'

Dr O'Connell points out that a mistaken diagnosis or normal changes in the body can make a natural recovery appear remarkable. He recalls one patient who had been referred for radiotherapy to treat what was thought to be ankylosing spondylitis, an inflammatory disease of the spine. After a brief course of treatment, the patient announced that he was no better and was not going to come in again. Three months later he did come back, and told the doctor that he was now much better. This was not the result of radiotherapy; he had been to an osteopath who had located a much less serious spinal problem which was the real cause of his distress.

Natural changes in the body's hormone balance can make cancer remit. Dr O'Connell had treated one woman with radiotherapy for advanced breast cancer. It was suggested that she should go into a hospice for her last few weeks of life. She went home instead. Three months later she returned alive and apparently quite fit, and X-ray examination showed only a ghost outline of her former metastases. Even tumours well outside the region which had been treated had now disappeared.

O'Connell thought this must be a remarkable spontaneous remission, until his chief pointed out that the sustained radiotherapy had precipitated an artificial menopause. When a woman enters the menopause certain hormones, which are involved with fertility but which also help to feed tumours, are no longer produced by the body. Within two years the woman's hormone balance had changed again and her cancer was back.

The medical profession is very wary of recoveries from cancer: for patients to be regarded as cured, the disease must have disappeared for at least five years. Tuberculosis is another fickle disease: it can come on very quickly, and it can remit just as fast. These things must be borne in mind when we assess the healer's claims.

If the healers' accomplishments only rarely fulfil the Lourdes criteria of a miracle, they are nonetheless amazing. Harry Edwards, the English healer, reported 281 cancer cases in his book *The Evidence for Spiritual Healing* in which tumours of various kinds had vanished or shrunk after the patient had received healing. Edwards invited doctors to examine and accompany patients at his healing sessions, and many admitted that the patients benefited in a remarkable and inexplicable way.

Bruce MacManaway, who practises and teaches healing in Fife, had a startling initiation into healing when, as a British Army officer on the beaches of Dunkirk, he found he could staunch the wounds of his injured men with the touch of a hand.

Gilbert Anderson, the Essex healer and secretary-general of the World Federation of Healing, was an RAF flying instructor in World War Two. He sustained a spinal injury which lost him the use of both legs and was told that he would spend the rest of his life in a wheelchair. His wife persuaded him to go to a healer who, much to Anderson's surprise, cured him.

'Not long after that,' he told me, 'my job took me round the country. By some chance, wherever I went I came into contact with desperately ill people. Within half an hour of my seeing them, they made remarkable recoveries. At first I thought it was coincidental, until it happened every day for several weeks.'

In 1975 the American healer Olga Worrall was invited to a medical symposium at Stanford University in California. Ten patients who had been thought incurable were brought to her by their doctors and given healing. Seven of those ten were subsequently cured or improved markedly. Mrs Worrall has literally scores of testimonies from doctors attesting to her ability to heal by laying on hands or praying for patients many miles away. Her psychic abilities can even help her diagnose illness in distant patients. Dr Norman Shealy relates that in the course of a telephone conversation she once told a patient's wife that her husband was not suffering from appendicitis, as his physician believed, but from gallstones. X-rays had not shown gallstones, but when the man was operated on the surgeon found over a hundred tiny stones. His appendix was all right.

Although it is the 'miracle cures' which get most publicity, most healers spend most of their time dealing with less dramatic complaints like skin disease and back pain. A lot of these conditions are psychosomatic or self-limiting – in other words, they might well disappear with time or if the patient stops feeling sorry for himself.

Nevertheless, it seems that a good healer does much more than offer a kind word and warm hand. Those incidents I described at the beginning of the chapter show that the healer appears to be giving off some form of energy. When a patient comes to Gilbert Anderson with a slipped disc, Anderson does not try to manipulate the spine. He lays his hand on the affected area and the disc just 'pops back into place'. Dr Michael Ash, a doctor who teaches healing in Cornwall, tells how he once fell into conversation with a stranger during a train journey. Unbeknown to Ash, his companion had damaged his knee in a motor accident several years earlier and had limped on a stiff leg ever since. They were sitting opposite each other, and Ash was leaning forward with his hands just a few inches from the injured knee. Suddenly 'the leg began to move about involuntarily', much to the concern of fellow passengers. This unexpected bout of 'automanipulation' restored the leg to full movement, and it has remained fit ever since, Ash says. In cases like this, where both healer and patient act involuntarily, something more than 'faith' or good intention is involved.

In the early 1960s Dr Bernard Grad, a psychiatrist at McGill University in Montreal, was introduced to a Hungarian healer, Colonel Oskar Estebany. Their meeting sparked off the longest series of laboratory experiments of healing ever attempted. Like many other talented healers, Mr Estebany was sufficiently convinced of his healing ability that he wanted it to be seriously investigated by an impartial scientist.

Harry Edwards had challenged the British medical profession to investigate his spiritual healing. Sadly, his self-assured manner succeeded in doing little but putting the doctors' backs up. Grad and Estebany were humble enough to realize they had mutually much to gain and little to lose by pooling their talents. Grad's background was Jewish and he says he was not particularly well acquainted with the healing tradition of Christianity.

Estebany told Grad that he had had some success in Hungary treating patients with thyroid problems. Grad had previously done research on the function of the thyroid gland, so it seemed natural to begin in that area.

Goitre, often known as 'Derbyshire throat', is a disease caused by lack of iodine in the diet. This deficiency causes the thyroid gland which is situated in the throat to swell. By feeding laboratory mice a low iodine diet and giving them small quantities of the drug thiouracil, which prevents iodine from reaching the thyroid, Grad was able to give them the disease.

From the outset the mice had been divided into three groups. All were kept in galvanized iron cages. One group was 'treated' by Mr Estebany, who, for fifteen minutes twice a day, five days a week, would hold his hands on the top and bottom of each animal's cage. The second group were just given their low iodine diet and thiouracil in their water and left to their own devices. The third group were given a heat treatment which consisted of warming their cages electrically to the same temperature which would have been achieved by Mr Estebany holding the cage.

After six weeks all groups of mice had goitre, but the disease was much less developed in the group which had been treated by Mr Estebany.

In the following experiment two groups of mice were made goitrous as before, but one group had pads of cotton wool which had previously been held by Mr Estebany placed in their cages. The other group just had untreated pads put in their cages. The group which had been given the pads treated by Estebany developed the disease less quickly.

In the third experiment the mice were given six weeks on the low iodine diet, by which time they were goitrous. They were then divided into two groups, one of which just got the heat treatment, while the others were treated by Mr Estebany holding their cages. During this time they had been returned to a normal diet. All the mice then began to lose their goitre, but the group treated by Mr Estebany did so much more swiftly.

Grad then experimented to see whether the healer could help skin wounds heal more efficiently. Mice were anaesthetized and a piece of skin about an inch square was removed from their backs with scissors. They were then divided into three groups, one getting healing, the second heat treatment and the third nothing. After fourteen days it was clear that the 'healed' mice had indeed healed more quickly than the others.

Subsequent experiments showed that the healer could also affect the growth of barley seedlings grown in the laboratory. Pots of seedlings were watered with a 1 per cent solution of salt in water. They were deliberately given salt water, which discourages plant growth, to put them 'in a state of need' which might be corrected by the healer. Dr Grad found that pots held by Mr Estebany yielded more and bigger seedlings than the untreated pots. He later found that the same effect could be achieved without the healer touching the pots at all. If Mr Estebany held a container of the saline, which was then fed to the plants, those seedlings would grow more strongly than those watered with untreated saline.

Dr Grad's work with Oskar Estebany aroused the interest of Sister Justa Smith, PhD, a Franciscan nun who is a bio-chemist and research director of the Human Dimensions Institute in Buffalo, New York. Justa Smith had been awarded her doctorate for research into the effect of electromagnetic fields on enzymes. Enzymes are the substances which cause chemical changes in the body, which in turn affect the growth and development of cells. Dr Smith speculated that if a healer really did have an effect on body chemistry, this effect should be measurable on enzymes. She invited Mr Estebany to her laboratory to do some more experiments.

For her experiments Dr Smith chose the digestive enzyme trypsin, which is produced in the pancreas. Its function is to break down proteins into amino-acids. The activity of en-zymes can only be measured by their effect on another substance, known as the substrate. The substrate in Dr Smith's experiments was chromogenic. The substrate changes colour as it breaks down, so the activity of the enzyme can be measured by taking samples of the solution and putting them in a spectrophotometer. A large batch of the enzyme solution was poured in equal proportions into four similar flasks. One flask was periodically subjected to a strong magnetic field of 8000–13,000 gauss. A second flask was treated by Mr Estebany who sat with his hands around it for an hour and a quarter. The third flask was left untouched to serve as a control. The fourth flask of enzymes was subjected to ultraviolet radiation, at a wavelength of 2537 Angströms. Ultraviolet light at this wavelength is known to damage enzymes, and the activity of the batch treated this way was reduced by 20 per cent. Dr Smith did this to see whether Mr Estebany could actually make the damaged enzymes repair themselves.

The experiments lasted a month with a fresh batch of

enzyme solution every day. At regular intervals samples were drawn from each flask and measured in the spectrophotometer. The results were surprising. They showed that the effect of Mr Estebany's hands was consistently almost exactly the same as that of the strong magnetic field. The enzyme activity in the untreated control flask remained at the anticipated normal level.

Bearing in mind that the earth's magnetic field is just 0.5 gauss, it was remarkable that Mr Estebany could be having an effect some 25,000 times greater. Of course, the fact that he was having the same effect as the magnetic field does not prove that he was emitting a magnetic field himself. You can crack a pane of glass with a hammer or with a sonic boom: the effect is similar but the cause is quite different. When Dr Smith used a magnetic detector to see if Mr Estebany was giving off a magnetic field, she got no reading at all.

Again, there was the possibility that the heat of the healer's hands could be having an effect. During her experiments Dr Smith got volunteers without any claimed healing powers to hold a flask as Mr Estebany had done. No significant change occurred, so heat seemed to be ruled out.

Mr Estebany's effect on the enzymes which had been damaged by ultraviolet radiation was perhaps even more remarkable. While he held the flask, samples were drawn off every fifteen minutes. After an hour the activity of the enzymes had been restored and the degenerative process halted. In other words, the healer was helping to put right a basic biochemical process – persuasive evidence that healing was a real physical phenomenon, not something that was 'all in the mind'.

Dr Smith did another series of experiments with three different healers to see if they could affect enzyme activity too. She found that they consistently accelerated the activity of some enzymes but decreased the activity of others. When they held flasks of the enzyme nicotinomide – adenine dinucleotide (NAD), for instance, the enzyme slowed up.

There are several thousand enzymes in the body, all with their own particular function, and this is no place to discuss their interaction. But Dr Smith suggests that a decreased production of NAD might actually be an advantage to a sick person because it would allow certain chemical processes involved in healing to take place more easily. If this is true, it seems that the hand healer instinctively but unconsciously boosts useful enzymes and discourages others. Incidentally, her healer volunteers had no idea which enzyme they were holding.

The encouraging results she had had with Mr Estebany made her want to repeat the experiments. Although the first series had been properly controlled and the results statistically significant, a repetition would make the evidence more convincing. Unfortunately for Dr Smith the second series was a failure. Mr Estebany was unable to achieve the same effects as before. At the time he was in the middle of a family crisis, it was midwinter in New York State, and he was not in very good health himself. Could this have affected his powers? It seemed a reasonable explanation but hardly enough to overcome Dr Smith's disappointment.

In his earlier experiments Bernard Grad had found that a healer improved the growth of barley seedlings by holding a bottle of the saline they were watered with. He had also found that a psychotic depressive patient appeared to retard their growth if he was asked to do the same thing: this suggests that a healthy state of mind could be crucial for the healer.

If we are prepared to accept that the laying on of hands does cause some kind of unidentified energy to flow from the healer to his patient or plant, what about distant healing? All the healers named so far in this chapter claim to have healed people many miles away by turning their thoughts towards them at regular intervals for a number of days.

In 1966 Dr Robert Miller, a chemical engineer and former professor at Georgia Tech, invited Olga Worrall and her husband Ambrose to join him in experiments to test whether the distant healing technique they had been using for fifty years could work on plants in laboratory conditions. The year before, a scientist working for the US Department of Agriculture had designed an instrument for measuring plant growth. An extremely lightweight lever is attached to the tip of the plant and connected to a rotary transducer. The device is sensitive enough to pick up movement as slow as a thousandth of an inch in an hour, and this is measured on a strip chart recorder.

For his experiments Dr Miller chose rye grass, which is a sturdy plant and grows rapidly. It was agreed that the Worralls should think of the rye grass seedlings in their prayers at nine o'clock in the evening of 4 January. The Worralls lived in Baltimore; Dr Miller's lab was 600 miles away in Atlanta.

On the evening of 4 January the laboratory was left locked with the tips of the seedlings attached to the recorder. The next morning Dr Miller examined the chart. He saw that until 9 pm the seedlings had been growing steadily at the rate of 0.00625 inches an hour. Preliminary studies had shown that this was the normal rate of growth for the seedlings in those conditions.

The chart showed that after nine o'clock, when the Worralls had begun their prayers, the trace had started to move upwards, and that by eight o'clock the next morning the growth rate had reached 0.0525 inches an hour – an increase over eleven hours of more than 800 per cent.

Like Dr Grad and Sister Justa Smith, Miller had established to his satisfaction that a healing energy existed. But he was no closer to identifying it.

Nuclear physicists who want to examine high energy particles sometimes use a device called a Cloud Chamber. The chamber is a glass cylinder about six inches high and six inches in diameter with a glass top which allows you to see what is going on inside. Methyl alcohol covers the bottom of the chamber to a depth of a quarter of an inch. When the chamber is placed on a block of dry ice, a vapour is formed by the alcohol and the air in the chamber. If a charged particle is passed through this vapour it leaves a visible trail of ionized molecules behind it.

A few years after their first experiment Mrs Worrall came to Miller's lab, where he had set up a cloud chamber. When she held her hands against the side of the chamber a wave pattern could be seen distinctly in the vapour. If she changed the position of her hands, the wave pattern would move round accordingly. None of Miller's colleagues were able to make any pattern appear in the mist when they did the same thing.

Mrs Worrall was able to affect the vapour at a distance too. In two subsequent experiments a camera was fixed above the glass top of the chamber. When Mrs Worrall, back home in Baltimore, directed her attention to the chamber, patterns similar to before appeared in the vapour and lasted several minutes.

In Britain the psychologist and electronics engineer Maxwell Cade has studied the brainwave activity of healers, psychics, yogis and Zen masters and has found strong similarities between them.

The cerebral hemispheres occupy the most space in the human brain and are far larger in man than in animals. In most people the left hemisphere of the brain dominates the right, though why we should have adopted this unilateral predominance is a puzzle. The right hemisphere has been associated, albeit rather loosely, with intuitive faculties. Cade finds that healers, psychics and people in meditation manifest similar amounts of activity in both hemispheres when they are wired up to an EEG. The frequency of their brainwaves is also markedly different from that of a normal person in the conscious waking state. In normal consciousness brainwave frequency is around fourteen to twenty cycles a second. When you daydream or relax with eyes closed, it falls to about ten cycles, and in deep sleep it falls to about three or four cycles.

The higher frequencies over thirteen cycles are called 'beta' rhythms, those between seven and thirteen 'alpha' rhythms, and those between four and seven cycles 'theta' rhythms. The lowest frequencies are called 'delta' rhythms.

Cade's psychic subjects manifest strong alpha and theta rhythms even in the waking state. When a healer and patient are both wired up to EEG machines, however, the healer's brain rhythms impose themselves on those of the patient. After a few minutes of laying on of hands strong alpha and theta rhythms can be recorded in the patient's brain which correspond very closely to the rhythms of the healer. In one of his experiments he found that an Indian swami could radically alter the brainwave patterns of students in his laboratory by just touching them lightly on the head. He induced a combination of high amplitude beta and theta rhythms, which in one case persisted for three days afterwards.

When an experienced consultant physician volunteered to be wired up to Cade's EEG, the machine only picked up left hemisphere beta wave activity. When the doctor was asked to think of himself trying to comfort a patient with an intractable disease, he began to show bilateral theta wave activity too.

Using biofeedback principles (more of this in Chapter Five), Cade finds that about one person in ten can be trained to develop 'healing rhythms'.

We are, of course, still no nearer to knowing just what energy is being transferred from healer to patient. Ripples in a cloud chamber and patterns on an EEG tell us that something is going on. But what is it?

The most controversial tool to be added to the psychic researcher's armoury in recent years is Kirlian photography. Named after the two Russian scientists who discovered the technique in 1939, Kirlian photography consists of photographing an object by placing it in direct contact with the film on a metal plate and passing a high frequency electric spark through the film on to the object. When the film is developed the outline of the object is seen surrounded by a halo or aura.

Russian parapsychologists and the American scientist Professor Thelma Moss suggest that it may indeed be a halo or aura which has been photographed. Psychics and mystics throughout history have said that all living things have an aura or haze of light surrounding them which intensifies or diminishes according to their physical and mental vitality.

The English healer Rose Gladden says that she has seen auras around people ever since she was a little girl. 'Imagine my mother's reaction,' she told a Wrekin Trust meeting in 1977, 'when I told her that everybody walked about in wonderful, colourful bubbles.'

When she heals, she finds that she is drawn to dark areas in the patient's aura which lie over the site of the disease. Kirlian photographs show that the fingers of healthy people are surrounded by a blue corona. If they are emotionally aroused the colour tends to change to red, white or yellow and develops a spiky pattern. When the finger-tips of a tired, emotionally depleted person are photographed, the corona appears patchy and shrunken.

Kirlian photographs of healers usually show more vigorous flares of bright colour around the finger-tips. After a healing session the aura is smaller and generally blue in colour. Conversely, the finger-tips of the patient who has received healing tend to show up brighter and bolder than before. Metal objects which have been handled by a healer emit a brighter Kirlian glow. A Kirlian photographer with a penchant for whole food has shown me photographs of slices of white sliced bread and wholemeal brown exposed to his high frequency spark. The sliced white was visible in bare outline, while the wholemeal brown flickered like the Northern Lights.

The effects of Kirlian photography have been dismissed by some as artefact, a trick of the spark. There are certainly many variables which could cause different patterns and colours to emerge. Sweat gland activity in the finger-tips could cause chemical changes sufficient to change the wavelength of reflected light. It would also alter the skin's conductivity and change the electrical climate of the photographic process.

Relaxation and meditation invariably lower skin conductivity, while emotional arousal raises it. It could be that Kirlian photography is another way of measuring galvanic skin potential – a kind of visual aid counterpart to the audio biofeedback instruments described in Chapter Five.

Kirlian photography might turn out to be a diagnostic aid like the electroencephalograph and the electrocardiograph. When the EEG and ECG were first introduced they were fraught with problems which have been ironed out after years of trial and error.

Another way to approach the idea of healing energy is to consider whether this energy, whatever it is, could be used for bad purposes as well as good. Dr Grad's experiments hinted that a mentally disturbed person could adversely affect the growth of plants, but Grad did not investigate this possibility more fully because he found it hard to get hold of disturbed patients to act as volunteers.

In *The Lancet* of 18 February 1978, Dr Anne Maguire, a dermatologist, reported two minor epidemics of skin disease which had broken out in Lancashire. The first outbreak occurred in a small ceramic factory among women whose job it was to hand paint pottery figures. Eight women had come out in severe irritant rashes, which they suspected were due to some unknown chemical in the materials they were handling.

Patch tests were made of all the women to see whether the rash could have been caused by an identifiable chemical. All the tests proved negative. The only woman who was suffering from a readily diagnosable skin disease had been off work intermittently for some time. When she was examined she was found to be an excitable personality, who, when asked to describe her illness, 'gave a vividly dramatic and verbose account, in which the small ceramic figures which she handled assumed the character of dangerous predatory beasts'. Significantly, she had been the first person to complain that the disease was caused by factory chemicals. But when all the women were invited to attend the clinic for patch tests, she did not attend. Later she did take the tests but protested that the negative results were wrong.

When the other seven women were told that the disease had no chemical origin but was probably due to their nervousness about the plight of their colleague, they accepted this explanation and their rashes disappeared completely.

The second outbreak affected sixteen employees in a textile factory. They had contracted an irritation of the skin and eyes, and they had put this down to a dye process. The factory inspector had found nothing suspect about the dying equipment and reported that other environmental safety regulations were being properly enforced.

When the workers were given patch tests, the results were all negative, except in one woman who was found to be sensitive to paraphenylene diamine, a chemical contained in certain hair dyes. She had been dying her hair for several years and had developed an allergy to this chemical. Paraphenylene diamine was not a constituent of any of the dyes she handled at work. One male worker had had mild chronic blepharitis, an inflammation of the eyelids, for several years, but his patch tests proved negative. It was this man and woman who had first suggested that factory chemicals were making them ill, and they had made a great fuss about it among their colleagues. But like the excitable lady in the first factory, they had been the last to turn up for skin tests at the clinic.

In both epidemics the symptoms of the original complainants were mimicked in their colleagues. 'The assumed cause,' Dr Maguire reported, 'became the direct focus of a generalized psychic contagion. spreading from the central couple, each of whom did have an unrelated, though organic condition.'

'The phenomena observed in these two outbreaks were common during the Middle Ages all over Europe. The phrase used to describe the condition was psychic possession. Some 500 years later, this term cannot be bettered.'

Here we are not dealing with a measurable 'energy' but with strong personalities who can convince others that they are likely to fall ill.

Earlier in this chapter I mentioned that many doctors ascribed the beneficial effects of healing to suggestion. Suggestion is a powerful tool in medicine; it is well known that almost any doctor with a moderately persuasive manner can make many of his patients' symptoms clear up for a while whether he gives them a powerful drug or some chemically inert substance. This phenomenon is called the *placebo* response (in Latin, placebo = I will please) and it is something which has to be taken into account when any form of medical treatment is being assessed. One patient in three, and sometimes the proportion is even greater, will respond well to a placebo treatment: pain will abate and other symptoms remit even though the patient has only been given a dummy pill or some other apparently useless form of therapy. Placebo effects can last up to six weeks or more, though they tend eventually to wear off.

Those factory epidemics suggest that the powers of suggestion can work the other way too. The resentful factory workers were effecting what we might call a *nocebo* (Latin, *I will hurt*) response in their colleagues.

One of the most potent and deliberate forms of suggestion is hypnotism. The hypnotist captures and holds the patient's complete attention and uses the opportunity to implant ideas and directions. In 1959 Drs Sinclair–Grieben and Chalmers reported in *The Lancet* how hypnotized patients had been induced to make warts on one side of their body disappear, while the warts on the other side stayed the same. More recently, Dr Richard Dreaper reported in the February 1978 issue of *The Practitioner* how he had successfully treated a middle-aged lady who had severe warts covering both her hands. After ten months of fortnightly hypnosis treatments only one wart remained. Dr Dreaper had deliberately suggested to his hypnotized patient that this one would remain while the others disappeared!

In Fort Worth, Texas, the radiotherapist Dr Carl Simenton has developed a therapy which encourages cancer patients to heal themselves. Simenton believes that cancer tends to attack people with a particular type of personality. The cancer personality 'shows a tendency to resent and an inability to express hostility; a tendency towards self-pity; difficulty in developing and maintaining meaningful, long-term relationships; and a poor "self-image".'

Carl Simenton had cancer himself when he was seventeen. 'I wish I could say that I did not have these traits at seventeen, but I know I did and still do residually,' he told the May Lectures' audience in London in 1975. 'It takes continuous effort on my own part to reduce their impact.'

Simenton does not take his patients off conventional medical treatment, but he does give them an additional therapy in which they are encouraged to visualize the tumours inside them being attacked by the medicines or X-rays they are receiving. The first patient on whom he tried this therapy had an extensive throat cancer, found it very difficult to swallow and had lost weight, having fallen to just seven stone. Simenton had given him a basic explanation of how a healthy body fights disease. He then got the man to relax three times a day and imagine hordes of white blood cells descending on his cancer and destroying it. The results were so encouraging that he has since used it on scores of patients with regular success. His method has strong similarities with Dr Norman Shealy's autogenic therapy for chronic pain (Chapter Six).

It has been taken up in Britain by Dr Ann Woolley-Hart, who has been doing group therapy with cancer patients since 1974. In the *British Homoeopathic Journal* of April 1977 she related how she had previously had to have a total hysterectomy because of malignant growth. She was advised to have radiotherapy to prevent further complications. As her own studies in radiobiology had convinced her that radiation messed up what natural defence mechanisms the body had against disease, she decided not to take their advice but to seek help elsewhere. She was treated by a homoeopathic physician and the healer Gilbert Anderson: five years later the cancer had not returned.

Dr Woolley-Hart now works with Gilbert Anderson. She teaches the patients simple biofeedback and relaxation techniques. They are told to imagine what their tumour looks like and then encouraged to think of it being overcome by the body's natural defence forces.

During the period of relaxation, Mr Anderson does laying on of hands, and the patients are asked to think of healing energy moving towards the site of the disease. At the end of the session the patients – there are usually six to eight in one group – discuss how they feel about the treatment and its effect. So far the results have been heartening, especially as many of the patients have only joined the group after being given six months or less to live. But as cancer is a horribly fickle disease and a 'cure' can only be pronounced five years after the disease has remitted, a full assessment cannot yet be published.

The National Federation of Spiritual Healers is a unique body in that its members are allowed to visit and treat patients in National Health Service hospitals. This privilege was granted them in the early 1950s – not long after the repeal of the old Witchcraft Act which made them liable to prosecution. In 1974 the Department of Health reconfirmed the privilege, making it clear that it only applied to members of the Federation on the condition that they did not try to interfere with medical treatment and came at the invitation of individual patients. The Federation runs training courses for fledgling healers which are backed up by correspondence course tuition in anatomy and physiology, meditation and absent healing.

Michael Endacott, the Federation's administrator, explained that courses are necessary not only for getting across practical advice but also to teach hospital regulations and the laws affecting the treatment of children. Enthusiastic novice healers have to be warned against vaunting their powers. 'We usually learn the patient's medical diagnosis at second-hand rather than from the doctor – and it does no good to go around making unjustified assertions.'

Healing does have its own kind of side effects too. Dr Arthur Bailey recalls a friend who found that he had 'the gift' and was anxious to try it on all and sundry. A close friend of his suffered from migraine, and the novice eagerly offered his help.

'The patient got rid of his migraine – but my friend picked it up. He was terrified. I have never seen anyone give up healing so quickly.'

The tiny amount of serious research which has been made of healing has raised more questions than it has answered. The sceptics who try to explain healing away as suggestion are obviously right to an extent. A great deal of successful healing doubtless is a placebo response. But then again, the placebo response is a remarkable phenomenon in itself; something which relieves one patient in three for quite long periods can hardly be dismissed as useless.

Personal experience and, more important, the laboratory evidence of Drs Grad and Smith do show that healers radiate some kind of energy which cannot only be felt but which also affects the most basic biological processes. What is that energy?

Many healers I have spoken with insist that the patient's desire to get better is as important as the healer's desire to cure. Whatever energy is given off by the healer must be 'internalized' by the patient; in other words, the healer only points the way for the patient to set his or her own natural restorative processes in operation.

Most puzzling of all is distant healing. We can choose to disbelieve the results of the once-off experiments by Dr Robert Miller. But if we accept that he, Mrs Worrall and the other doctors and scientists involved in such experiments are not blatant liars, we have to accept that telepathy operates between humans and plants. The next chapter, on radionics, will serve only to confuse you further.

2 Radionics—Open the Box

When we go to the doctor for a medical examination we expect to be prodded, thumped, hit on the knee with little hammers and asked to pee into a bottle. Most of us do not have much idea why the doctor should want to do these things, but they are familiar rituals and therefore we trust them.

If, on the other hand, the doctor did none of these things but took a pair of scissors, snipped off a lock of your hair and swung a pendulum over it, you might start to wonder whether you had come to the right place. If he then told you that you would not have to come and see him again because he would be 'broadcasting' your medicine through the ether with the help of a little black box, you might think it was time for him to retire from practice – and for you to retire from his surgery double quick.

In fact most of the doctors who did this sort of thing have retired. In Britain only a handful of doctors now practice 'radiesthesia' and radionics. But the technique appears to be more popular than ever with lay practitioners. The Radionics Association has more than 50 members and claims that at any time about 5000 people are receiving radionic treatment.

Radiesthesia is a long word for dowsing, that apparently extra-sensory method of finding underground springs. The water diviner with his forked hazel twig is a familiar historical figure. More recently the Marathon Oil Company employed a dowser to look for oil wells. But as no one, the dowser included, has yet come up with an explanation of how it works, some people are inclined to believe that it is a mixture of hoax and guesswork.

It is difficult to dismiss dowsing out of hand if you have actually done it yourself. I found that I was able to locate underground water pipes at my first attempt at dowsing; and expert dowsers claim that 50 per cent of us have the knack. Why the other 50 per cent should *not* have the knack is hard to say; the ability to dowse may be akin to having an ear for music or an eye for colour.

Dowsing is not confined to water divining. It is used for finding precious metals, lost objects and – what interests us here – medical diagnosis.

Radionics is a kind of mechanical dowsing, in which the instrument used for diagnosis can also be used to treat the patient. The instrument is popularly known as 'The Black Box' and usually consists of a number of dials and knobs on the outside, which are connected to a series of magnets and potentiometers on the inside. Some instruments are plugged into the main, others are not. None of the instruments make any sense in conventional electromagnetic terms, and some practitioners have given up their boxes altogether, preferring to plug themselves directly into the 'subtle energy' fields which are the basis of their healing theory. A few collaborate with sympathetic doctors, who refer intractable patients for radionic treatment and accept referrals in return.

As radionics is surely the most outlandish of all alternative medical therapies, the doctors who do believe in it do not go out of their way to advertise the fact to their orthodox colleagues, especially if they work in the National Health Service. Dr Alec Forbes, a consultant physician who works in Plymouth, is one exception to this rule.

He has referred difficult cases for radionic treatment and has allowed one patient to be kept in a hospital bed while his local radionic practitioner tried her distant healing techniques. The patient suffered from a complicated condition, and drug therapy would have offered more problems than solutions, he told me. By keeping the patient in hospital he was able to keep him under observation while the radionic practitioner did her work miles away.

Dr Forbes has used medical dowsing as a diagnostic aid for over ten years. He takes a lock of the patient's hair or a spot of blood. Then, with his mind 'in neutral', he lets a pendulum swing over the patient's sample while he mentally poses a series of questions which can be answered by a Yes or a No. If the answer is Yes, the pendulum will rotate clockwise, if No, anticlockwise. If the pendulum simply swings to and fro in no particular direction, the answer is 'Yes, but . . .' 'Perhaps', or 'You have phrased the question wrongly'. The pendulum is used for diagnosis and for choosing the correct medicine for the patient.

Just where these answers come from is a bit of a mystery. All dowsers stress that you should not concentrate too hard. Dowsing appears to operate through some intuitive facility, and bringing too much thought to bear on the subject can throw up wrong answers. It has been suggested that water divining relies on the dowser picking up some kind of electromagnetic signal which comes up through the earth. This explanation cannot be true because experienced dowsers can locate their object at a distance or even from a map. It certainly does not explain how you can diagnose illness from a lock of hair.

Dr Arthur Bailey, a senior lecturer in electrical engineering at Bradford University and president of the British Society of Dowsers, has practised medical and geological radiesthesia for twelve years. He first learnt about dowsing by reading a library book given him while he was lying in bed recovering from a prolonged bout of 'flu. He had been 'as sceptical as the next man' about the subject but decided to see if he could do it. The first thing he found was the stopcock to the house water main. No one had been able to locate it before, and Bailey found it was nowhere near the spot indicated on the house plans. He went on to find an old drainage system which lay long forgotten under the front drive.

When his interest and skill at dowsing had become well known locally, the Post Office commissioned him to look for concealed mine shafts which were thought to lie on the proposed path of a new telephone cable. The contractors had already nearly lost one excavator when it capsized into an old capped shaft, and they had been unable to find any instrument which could detect other similar hazards.

Dr Bailey used a standard method of dowsing by cross-reference. The dowser divides his terrain into a square and walks up one side until he gets a twitch on his dowsing rods. He then walks down an adjacent side until he gets another twitch. By taking a grid cross-reference you should alight on the object you are looking for.

He located seven old shafts on the site, but fortunately none lay in the path of the cable. Of those seven at least four were indisputably in the spot he had predicted, because subsequent examination of the site showed that there were indentations in the ground where subsidence had already occurred. One of the contractor's men, who had not tried dowsing before, borrowed Bailey's rods to see if he could find anything. He was surprised to come across what appeared to be a horizontal hole under the surface, which Bailey had missed. It turned out to be a mine gallery. Bailey had missed it because he had only been expecting to find vertical shafts.

'When I started dowsing I thought it must be the result of some force coming up out of the ground. I had heard of map dowsing, but thought it was quite ridiculous. But I did some experiments on an archaeological site and found that I could locate objects by standing at the side and letting someone else walk over the area.'

Subsequent experiments showed that he could pick up such reactions at a distance and way out of sight of the terrain. When he ran a course for beginners in 1977 he presented them with the plans of his house and garden and told them to try and find the water and drainage systems by swinging a pendulum over the paper. Six of the thirty students located both mains and drains spot on, and this was their first attempt at map dowsing.

Most of Dr Bailey's dowsing is medical. 'I found there were many more people who were ill than needed wells.' The great majority of his patients have back trouble which has not responded to orthodox medical treatment. He locates the displaced disc or vertebra by letting a pendulum swing over the spine and slowly moving it downwards and allowing the pendulum to give a clear answer to each bone. He has developed a manipulative technique which is a blend of chiro-practice and hand healing but which he has largely taught himself by dowsing.

The pendulum can tell you whether it is right to manipulate and how you should set about it. The first time I got a patient with a twisted sacro-iliac joint, I was terrified. There she was stretched out on the couch, and I was ex-pected to do something. I took out the pendulum and asked: 'Can I correct this?' The pendulum swung clockwise – Yes. Then I asked: 'Should I do it today?' Yes, again. After a series of questions I finished up with one leg up on the couch, my arm flung round her back and my fingers on the offending vertebra. I got her to breathe deeply, and she breathed out and then I pressed with my fingers and gave a little twist. The pendulum told me that the joint had gone back, and there was a lot of heat coming off her back, which is generally a sign that the bone has gone back into place.

Dr Bailey now uses that technique regularly, though he is careful not to use much force. 'It looks like an osteopathic manipulation, but I dare not put as much force into it as an osteopath would. If you are not trained, you have to be careful.'

Radiesthesia has flourished sufficiently to have two small medical societies devoted to its pursuit. The older of the two, the Medical Society for the Study of Radiesthesia, appears to be almost moribund and now has considerably fewer members than thirty years ago. Its present Hon. Sec. is a homoeopath, Dr Marianne Harling, who admits that she was never very good at dowsing herself.

'It does not go very well with a scientific training. You tend to be far too critical, and the pendulum will not work for you. Radiesthesia often works best for a husband and wife team: the scientific doctor asks the questions, while his artistic wife swings the pendulum.'

The more active body is the Psionic Medical Society which also only admits doctors and dentists and is somewhat contemptuous of the efforts of the medically unqualified radionic practitioners.

Two founder members of the Society, the surgeon George Laurence and dentist Carl Upton, published a book called *Psionic Medicine* in 1974 to explain their work. Like the homoeopathic doctors they insist that only medically trained individuals can be trusted to practise psionic medicine. Apart from a theoretical outline, they refuse to reveal what the practice of psionic medicine actually entails:

> Extensive experience in psionic medicine leaves no doubt of the need to bring to light the inherent danger of use of the pendulum without recourse to valid knowledge . . . The path of dowsing is strewn with increasing numbers of unfortunate people who have strayed into a cloud-cuckoo land of fantasy and brought nothing but folly and worthless escapism into their lives: and if they have undertaken to help others, as they so often feel constrained to do by virtue of their own emptiness and need for self-justification, the results for their charges can be equally tragic . . . It is for this reason that the Psionic Medical Society steadfastly refuses to publish detailed formulations of its techniques.

If one delves deeper into the history of the Psionic Medical Society one realizes that the authors want things both ways. Like the Faculty of Homoeopathy they are obviously keen to maintain links with orthodox medicine, despite the ideological differences. One way of keeping up the appearance of respectability is to make a show of condemning the unqualified. Nevertheless, the Society has been quite prepared to recruit expert dowsers who are laymen as consultants or associate members so that it can draw from their talents.

Disputes about the possible dangers of radiesthetic medicine have racked the Radionics Association too. In 1977 a German radionic practitioner, Karl Scheller, tried to convince members of the Association that their methods were 'open to attack' from black magicians. Scheller proposed that they adopt his own form of radionic practice which involved a stylized ritual and the protective presence of a guru to ensure that malign influences could not penetrate their broadcasts. Few members of the Radionic Association took his warning seriously, though the Secretary, John Wilcox, did. Wilcox subsequently resigned his post in protest.

The founder of radionics was a San Francisco physician, Dr Albert Abrams. He had enjoyed a successful career in orthodox medicine in the early part of this century. As a student he had won the gold medal at Heidelberg University, and at the age of 30 he was professor of pathology at Stanford University and president of the San Francisco Medico-Chirurgical Society.

One day he was examining a middle-aged male patient by percussing his abdomen. Percussion is a standard diagnostic technique: by tapping parts of the body with one finger, the doctor can judge from the note given off whether the organs underneath are healthy. A tap on the chest above a healthy lung, for instance, should result in a clear, resonant note. Dr Abrams found that the note given off by his patient's abdomen was dull and flat, but only on one spot. The patient was not suffering from any internal disorder which could explain this dull note. His problem was a growth on the lip.

Although he had no diagnostic precedent for so doing, Abrams attributed the dull note to this growth and decided to experiment further. The most bizarre aspect of this dull note was that it only appeared when the patient faced West! Abrams percussed the abdomina of several other patients suffering from a variety of complaints, and found that when they faced West, dull notes could be elicited by percussing particular spots. Gradually he built up a diagnostic map of the abdomen: different diseases had their own dull spot. For example, a dull note from a central spot just above the navel indicated some kind of cancer, while a dull note at bottom left was a sure sign of malaria.

Abrams leapt to the conclusion that diseases must be emitting some form of electromagnetic radiation. To test this idea he got healthy volunteers to hold glass containers of diseased tissue in their hands while their abdomen was percussed. He got the same results as before. Holding the diseased tissue made a dull note appear on the same spot as if the volunteer was suffering from the disease himself. He went on to connect his volunteers by wires to containers on the other side of the room. The technique still worked.

Now his only problem was that the human abdomen was too small: the dull spot of certain diseases overlapped. The cancer spot coincided with the syphilis spot, for instance. A tricky problem.

Having decided that he was dealing with an electromagnetic phenomenon, Abrams put a variable resistor on the wire connecting patient with tissue. When he percussed the cancer/syphilis spot he would only get the dull note for cancer when the theostat was set at a resistance of 50 ohms, while the syphilis only showed up at a resistance of 55 ohms. He subsequently found that if the tissue samples were replaced by samples of hair, blood or sputum from a diseased patient, his diagnosis was still quite accurate.

Abrams could not believe that the 'electrical reactions' he had discovered were just a diagnostic aid. If disease was an alteration in the electromagnetic field, then it should be curable by electromagnetic methods, he thought. He designed a machine which he called 'The Oscilloclast' which was reported to subject the patient to '200 electrical charges a minute interspersed with radio-frequency electromagnetic impulses'. He claimed great success for this machine.

Unfortunately for his reputation he embarked on a large sales campaign, leasing and selling his instruments to anyone who showed an interest. They were eagerly copied by bandwagonning quacks, and 'magic boxes' appeared all over the United States and Europe. What might have been a boon to the medical profession was soon overtaken by notoriety.

Abrams died in 1924, shunned by most of his colleagues. Nevertheless, his claims had already made enough impact in Britain for the Royal Society of Medicine to sponsor an investigation into his diagnostic method. Using a device called the Emanometer, which was very similar to Abrams's diagnostic box, Dr W. E. Boyd of Glasgow University and Dr C. B.

Heald of the Civil Aviation Authority conducted a series of tests under the surveillance of a committee chaired by Sir Thomas (later Lord) Horder. We will hear more of Dr Boyd in Chapter Three, on homoeopathy.

Two working-class lads from the Gallowgate district of Glasgow were recruited as volunteers: one of them was trained to percuss, while the other obligingly lent his abdomen. Tests were made of samples of the patient's blood and sputum.

The first series of tests showed that the emanometer was pretty reliable. In 64 trials diagnosis was correct 46 times and inaccurate 18 times. The odds against getting such a result by chance were calculated as 3037 to 1.

A second series of tests was less successful, but Dr Boyd protested that the samples were old and probably contaminated. In a further series of tests Dr Boyd was asked to use his instrument to differentiate between bottles of white powder. Some of them had had a few drops of homoeopathically prepared water added to them, while the others were untreated. To all appearances the powder in each bottle was exactly the same. But Boyd managed to pick out the treated bottles of powder with 100 per cent accuracy.

Horder and his committee were not interested in substantiating any claims for homoeopathy, but they had to report to the Royal Society of Medicine that the diagnostic potential of the emanometer had been 'established to a very high degree of probability'. While Horder could not find fault with Dr Boyd, he expressed much misgiving about the way Abrams had conducted his research and sold his instruments to all and sundry. Abrams's technique had not fared well in experiments made in the United States under the eye of a team of observers chosen by *Scientific American* magazine. Its disreputable image was not dispelled, and no more research was performed by official medical organizations either side of the Atlantic.

Today radionic practitioners have forsaken Abrams's electromagnetic theory in preference to the idea that disease is the result of disturbances in 'subtle energy' fields, which surround and permeate the physical body. They regard the physical body as just one part of a spectrum of life energy. Subtle energy is not caught like the physical body in space and time. Like the water which can be located on the dowser's map, disturbances in the subtle energy field can be picked up by swinging a pendulum over a lock of hair, spot of blood or even a photograph of the patient.

Although they have abandoned the electromagnetic theory, most radionic instruments consist of a crypto-electrical circuitry of magnets and variable resistors. Some are described in the sales literature as 'magnetically energized'. There are at least four different British manufacturers of radionic instruments.

The instrument is operated by placing the patient's sample, or 'witness' as it is called in the trade, on to a metal plate or well. The operator then swings a pendulum over the witness and turns a dial until he gets a 'Yes' answer from the pendulum. Instruments vary in the number of dials they have; some have three or four, others as many as twenty-four. The dials are generally numbered with a scale from 1 to 10.

Once the operator has got a reading for each dial, he consults a 'rate book' to decide how the dials should be reset to broadcast a health restoring energy field back to the patient.

Some instruments come equipped with batches of sealed phials containing samples of diseased tissue. The operator makes his diagnosis by placing phials on the instrument with the 'witness' until the pendulum gives a 'Yes' answer. A suitable remedy might then be found by taking a batch of homoeopathic preparations and putting them through the same pendulum question and answer routine. The potion thus selected might then be given to the patient in some physical form or put into the well of the instrument and 'broadcast' paraphysically.

The black box must be one of the biggest obstacles to radionics being taken more seriously. Some patients may be impressed if they are shown a bewildering piece of technology, but I for one would find it easier to accept the idea of healing by extra-sensory perception if it did not also appear to rely on pseudo-electronic gadgetry for its efficacy.

The manufacturers themselves tend to be circumspect about the powers of their instruments. The sales literature for one brand includes caveats that 'the operation of this instrument is dependent on the radiaesthetic sensitivity of the user'. And John Wilcox pointed out that 'a radionic instrument alone can do nothing. It is as good as its user and is of secondary importance. Non-physical energy can only be monitored by the human psychoneural system'.

Dr Arthur Bailey made his own radionic box for distant healing which he called his 'grey box'. It has dials on the outside, connected to spindles. Apart from that it is quite empty.

'A woman in the United States,' he told me, 'was had up for selling boxes filled with sawdust. But they worked all right.' He suggests that the dials on a box are just a way of coding information, rather like writing a thought down in words on a piece of paper.

Radionic practitioners who make and use boxes reply that it may be all right for acutely sensitive dowsers like Bailey to dispense with instruments. He can work like a brilliant orchestra conductor who remembers every part of a symphony without consulting the score. Less proficient operators need devices and charts to help them keep their thoughts together.

The analogy with thoughts and words or music and the printed score has been taken up by other medical dowsers, notably Dr Aubrey Westlake of Hampshire. Westlake's theory is that health has a pattern and that by broadcasting a suitable pattern to patients they can be restored to health.

The sixteenth-century mystic and herbalist Paracelsus wrote that 'all natural forms bear their signature, which indicate their true nature . . . This signature is often expressed in the exterior forms of things, and by observing that form we may learn something in regard to their interior qualities'. This notion is the basis of sympathetic magic and explains why man-shaped plants like ginseng and the mandrake have been thought to have cure-all properties. The spiritual significance of pattern and shape also preoccupied the Egyptians who designed the Pyramids and the Greek architects who built their temples in the proportions of the 'golden mean' with a height-to-width ratio of 1:1.618.

By the question and answer dowsing technique Westlake came to the conclusion that coloured shapes drawn on paper in the ratio of 1:3 or 2:5 propelled energy centrifugally. If the patient's witness were placed at a particular point on one of these patterns together with a homoeopathic remedy, the energy of the remedy would be broadcast automatically to the patient. With some patterns only the name of the remedy had to be written on the paper to achieve the same effect. Nearly 300 people were treated by this method and allegedly benefited from it. [*The Pattern of Health*, Aubrey Westlake (Shambhala, 1973)].

Malcolm Rae, who has worked with Dr Westlake and is one of the most prolific manufacturers of radionic instruments, has worked out patterns for homoeopathic remedies consisting of lines drawn radially from the centre of a circle. These patterns are printed on white card and inserted into a special radionic instrument. Rae compares his cards to gramophone records and the instrument to a gramophone. The groove on a record contains a pattern of the recorded sound. If you looked along the groove you could see the pattern; but you could not hear the music without the instrument.

Radionics literature is not short of case histories documenting successful treatments. Most patients turn to radionics when they have had no luck with orthodox medicine. John Wilcox, the former secretary of the Radionics Association, first became interested in the subject when a radionic practitioner apparently cured his cystitis which had not yielded to months of conventional treatment. Chronic conditions are the radionic practitioner's staple fare.

In the terms of orthodox science this kind of evidence is merely anecdotal, and radionic practitioners have shown little inclination to make it appear more convincing. John Wilcox tried to persuade all the practising members of the Radionics Association to submit records of their treatments and assess whether they had been successful, partly successful or failures. Even this informal attempt at collecting evidence roused meagre enthusiasm, and few bothered to respond.

Success in radiesthesia is possibly rather difficult to compare directly with conventional medical methods. The practitioner is acting on the 'subtle body' rather than the physical body and may get very different readings from the former than the conventional doctor might get from the latter. A member of the Medical Society for the Study of Radiesthesia dowsed a diagnosis of 'flu from a patient known to have a duodenal ulcer. The patient did not get 'flu till two days later. On another occasion a radiesthetist working with Dr Westlake announced that a patient had 'improved' shortly after he had in fact died. Westlake expressed concern at this faulty diagnosis, only to be told that it was not faulty. Physical death, he was told, had liberated the subtle body, which was almost certainly feeling a lot better for it.

Radiesthetic diagnosis is easily ridiculed by sceptics. Abrams himself is reported to have been caught out by doctors who sent him blood samples from chickens and rabbits, which he variously diagnosed as suffering from cancer, venereal disease, diabetes and malaria. And in the magazine *World Medicine* in May 1977, Dr David Delvin related how he had tricked a radionic practitioner into believing that a snip of cat's fur was a human sample. Delvin sent the sample with a letter written under an assumed name, giving details of symptoms which any doctor would recognize as those of diabetes. The radionic practitioner apparently took little account of the symptoms Delvin described but wrote back to say he was suffering from disturbances in the small and large intestines and the nervous system.

In fact Delvin admitted that his cat *did* have worms and had been 'a bit neurotic', so the practitioner's analysis had been reasonably accurate. As far as Dr Delvin was concerned, however, the practitioner had made a fool of himself by not recognizing the symptoms of diabetes.

The attempts by radionic practitioners to have themselves taken more seriously have not been helped by the activities of individuals like the self-styled Dr Bruce Copen. Copen, who lives in Sussex, is a manufacturer of radionic instruments and author of several books and pamphlets on dowsing and radiesthesia. In the blurbs to his books he describes himself as a doctor of philosophy, doctor of letters and sports a number of other fancy sounding titles. Dr Copen's literary and entrepreneurial exercises have not endeared him to the Radionics Association, which refuses to admit him as a member. The association's antipathy has less to do with his skill as a dowser than with his academic pretensions. The doctorates which he claims to hold are not awarded by any university; they are in fact quite spurious. When I asked him to name the institutions which had granted him his degrees, he simply described them as 'organizations which approve of me and my work'. Not content with awarding himself degrees, Copen has also been in the business of selling them too, though he told me that he had now given up this profitable diploma mill.

Radionics is not the only fringe medical therapy beset by dubious operators with even more dubious qualifications. Acupuncture has more than its fair share of doctors and professors who have found that it's easier to get a degree by awarding it to yourself than by studying in the boring old conventional manner.

Radionic practitioners reject the idea of meeting conventional medicine on its own ground by doing controlled experiments and trials because, they argue, they would be working at cross purposes. Even the medically qualified radiesthetists profess a dislike of formal scientific procedures performed under the eyes of sceptical observers. George Laurence and Carl Upton write that:

It has been known for a sceptical doctor to refer a case for psionic medical diagnoses as a sort of test; perhaps even to discredit the technique. This scepticism conveys itself to the practitioner, either directly or through the patient, and unless he is able to preserve his integrity of mind, failure is inevitable . . . It therefore behoves every practitioner . . . to avoid any occasion where there is likely to be a climate of disbelief.

This attitude first struck me as unnecessarily pompous and defensive, but Dr Arthur Bailey suggested that it might not be unreasonable. He once did an informal experiment to see whether an 'unsympathetic observer' could affect his dowsing skill. He knew that a stream ran under the garden of a house where he was staying. He asked his sister-in-law to watch him dowsing for this stream. He planned to make several surveys and told his sister-in-law that sometimes she should imagine him finding the stream and during the other surveys she should imagine him not finding the stream. She was not to tell him which way she was thinking. In the event, whenever she thought of him finding the stream he did find it, and whenever she imagined that he would not find it. he did not.

Dr Alec Forbes is the only NHS doctor who has tried to have radionic therapy put to the test of a formal clinical trial. It did not fail due to the scepticism of observers; it was never allowed to take place because the local medical committee deemed it 'unethical'.

If you do not believe in extra-sensory faculties and subtle bodies, you might assume that radionics was at worst a harmless pastime. But medical and lay practitioners of the art insist that it is not safe in the hands of the uninitiated. Malcolm Rae admitted to me that his mistakes have occasionally made patients worse. David Tansley, a chiropractor and leading radionic theorist, gave up using his instrument when he found that he was taking on his patients' symptoms himself.

The Radionics Association takes the risk of iatrogenic disease seriously enough to insist that all practitioners take out accident insurance. Annual premiums run at about £25 for £25,000 cover – but you may be relieved to learn that no British radionic practitioner has yet been sued for malpractice.

The phrase 'all in the mind' usually conveys the idea that something is imaginary, contrived or false. That idea is the result of our traditional notion that mind and matter are separate phenomena. But you do not have to be an enthusiast of the paranormal to perceive that mind and matter are not separate, especially in the medical field. Emotional upsets can cause physical disease, and as we shall see in later chapters on biofeedback and autogenics, physical disease can be dispersed by mental exercise.

Practitioners of radionics and distant healing might take this a step further. They would argue that quite literally everything is in the mind, that we are not all individual little minds separate from each other but part of a universal consciousness, a global mind. If this is the case, the idea of mental energy flowing from one person to another or from one thing to another should seem no more extraordinary than blood flowing from the heart to the toes and back again. (In fact even this idea was itself considered extraordinary when Harvey first proposed it only 350 years ago.)

The trouble with applying revolutionary ideas, however attractive they may appear, is that it upsets everybody's comfortable habits. And if comfortable livelihoods are at stake too, the revolutionary needs beware. Ridicule and ostracism meet every innovator who threatens his colleagues' bank balance, as the founder of homoeopathy, the subject of the next chapter, discovered for himself.

3 Homoeopathy—Shaken, Not Stirred

In May 1977 I was commissioned by the *Observer* magazine to write a large feature article on alternative medicine. It was to cover all the principal unorthodox therapies, ranging from the widely accepted, like osteopathy, to the frankly arcane, like radionics.

Knowing that the Queen had startled conventional medical opinion some years previously by appointing a homoeopathic doctor, Margery Blackie, as one of the Royal Physicians, it seemed like a good idea to approach this lady for an interview. Sad to say, I never managed to meet her. When I explained to her assistant that I was writing about alternative medicine and wanted to include homoeopathy in my article, it was made abundantly clear to me that I had committed a *faux pas*. 'Homoeopathy is not part of some alternative medicine,' I was firmly told. 'It is *the* alternative medicine. The Alternative to Allopathy. If you wish to write about homoeopathy, that is all very well. But it is not to be associated with other therapies practised by unqualified people.'

I was well and truly put in my place.

Royal patronage has been a great morale booster for the homoeopaths. If most people today know nothing else about homoeopathy, they have probably heard somewhere of the Queen's interest in the subject. Dr Blackie is the latest in a line of homoeopathic physicians who have been appointed to the Royal Family. King George VI was attended by Sir John Weir and even named one of his racehorses after a homoeopathic remedy, Hypericum. And according to Buckingham Palace's official spokesperson, the present Queen has not maintained the connection just for the sake of tradition; she does actually consult Dr Blackie and take treatment for occasional physical ailments.

Many patients who have been drawn to homoeopathy defend it with the zeal of a religious convert. But like the convert, their beliefs are usually based less on hard science than on faith and personal experience. Royal patronage may convince some people, but it carries little weight in scientific circles, where homoeopathy has long been ridiculed for its principles which run quite against those of conventional medicine.

The idea of allopathy is that you treat disease with drugs which have an opposite effect to the disease's symptoms. The major symptom of arthritis, for instance, is inflammation, and it is treated allopathically by prescribing a drug like aspirin which wages war against the substances which cause inflammation. In homoeopathy you do not treat disease, you treat the patient; and you treat him with tiny doses of medicines which would normally produce similar symptoms to those he is complaining about.

If that seems paradoxical, the second principle of homoeopathy is even more bewildering. Whereas the orthodox doctor tends to treat more severe complaints by giving a higher dose of the drug, the homoeopath does the opposite. His most powerful remedies are extreme dilutions.

To understand why the homoeopaths should want to stand conventional wisdom on its head, we have to know a little about the history of their movement. The principle that 'like cures like' is as ancient as medicine. In fact it is part of magical lore which claims that a herb shaped like an ear will cure earache, or that a red flower like burnett, which is the same colour as dried blood, can heal wounds. Homoeopaths do not profess to be practitioners of sympathetic magic, however. They take their lead from a German physician called Samuel Hahnemann, who was born in Saxony in 1755.

The son of a tyrannical father who was determined that his son should be an academic success, Hahnemann got used to hard work at an early age. By his mid-thirties he was a highly respected physician and very well read. Like many great innovators his quest for knowledge was fuelled by his dissatisfaction with the prevailing professional standards of the day. He came to regard much of what passed as medicine as little better than licensed butchery and poisoning, and was particularly distressed by the ham-fisted way his colleagues prescribed their remedies.

In 1790 he was translating a leading British textbook, Cullen's *Materia Medica*, into German. He was puzzled by the author's explanation of the way cinchona bark, the source of quinine, relieved fevers like malaria. Quinine was widely used for treating 'the ague' and Hahnemann suspected that it was being overprescribed so much that it was doing more harm than good to ague sufferers.

It had been reported that workers on the farms in South America where cinchona was grown suffered from symptoms very like those of malaria. This seemed strange. Why should a drug which undoubtedly relieved fever also seem to cause it, or something very much like it?

Hahnemann decided to experiment. He dosed himself with half an ounce of cinchona bark twice a day for several days. And he found that after a week he had the symptoms of malaria. In other words, a drug which could cure sick people could make the symptoms of disease appear in a healthy person. This observation was to be the cornerstone of homoeopathy.

Quinine has fallen out of use this century largely because it produces the side-effects which Hahnemann was worried about. In very high doses it can cause headache, vomiting, fever, excitement, confusion, deafness, blindness and abortion. Regular medical doses can cause noises in the ears, nausea, stomach pains, headaches and rashes. And if it is taken by people who have had malaria for some time it can give them a worse disease, blackwater fever, in which red blood cells are destroyed and the patient's urine turns black.

Hahnemann had seen many patients suffering as much from the ravages of the drug as they had from the original disease. This prompted him to try prescribing it in ever smaller doses. Not only did his patients suffer fewer side-effects but – curiouser and curiouser – the smaller the dose he gave, the better they recovered from their illness. He could not explain this phenomenon – indeed, 150 years later his followers are still trying to come up with an explanation to satisfy their orthodox colleagues – but it worked for him.

Hahnemann finally came to the conclusion that symptoms were the body's way of fighting disease. The allopaths, who set themselves the task of attacking the symptoms, were going about things the wrong way. The physician's job should be to help the body win the fight, and the best way to do this was to give a tiny dose of a substance which could mimic those symptoms in a healthy person.

His experience with cinchona bark led him to try similar experiments on other substances. The herbals of the day contained as many remedies as pharmaceutical drug compendia do today, and he set about testing these substances on himself and other healthy volunteers.

Belladonna, he found, produced very similar symptoms in a healthy person to scarlet fever. Aconite aroused feelings of persecution. They should therefore be used to treat those complaints in the sick. In his tests, which he called 'provings', he did not content himself with noting the major effects of the substance. He would get his volunteers to report the least changes in their physical and mental state, their dietary habits, their reactions to the weather, their family relationships and sleeping habits. Vast quantities of data were collected, and he found that each substance had its own distinct effects. Some of these effects cropped up in all the volunteers, some in a proportion, and others in only a few. No detail was regarded as too insignificant.

The diversity of remedies, he decided, was similar to the diversity between human beings. Some remedies actually seemed to have a personality of their own which could be matched with types of patient. Sulphur, for instance, made his provers feel hot and sweaty, and suffer from heartburn, boils and body odours; they would get impatient and irritable and become intolerant of sultry weather.

Many of his patients reacted the same way when they were

ill. Whatever the pathology of their complaint might have been, these symptoms would occur time and again. This made him think that the disease was much less important than the patient. The same disease would bring different symptoms in different types of person. The answer was not to attack the disease with a specific remedy but to treat the patient himself. If that patient reacted to disease by feeling hot, irritable, smelly and dyspeptic, he should be given a homoeopathic dose of sulphur to help him in his struggle.

Hahnemann's new theory elicited little enthusiasm from most of his medical colleagues, who regarded the whole business as laughable. Apothecaries cared for homoeopathy even less. Hahnemann had taken to preparing his own medicines by his own methods, which was not good for their business. And when they learnt that he was advocating tiny doses they came to the conclusion that he was out to ruin them financially.

Some doctors were sympathetic, however. The London physician Frederick Foster Quin went to study under Hahnemann and brought homoeopathy over to Britain. Quin had a number of aristocratic friends who formed the basis of this practice, and this new approach quickly gained social cachet. But the eminence of Quin's clientele enraged other senior physicians, notably one John Ayrton Paris, who was later to become president of the Royal College of Physicians.

Paris did his damnedest to have Quin denounced as a quack and barred from practice. In 1850 Quin had founded a homoeopathic hospital in London's Golden Square and had attracted several colleagues to work with him. In 1854 the city was hit by an epidemic of cholera, and Quin's hospital was enlisted as a treatment centre. The death rate from cholera in those days was between 50 and 75 per cent. During that 1854 outbreak over half the patients in hospital with cholera died – except at the homoeopathic hospital where mortality was 16 per cent, only one patient in six. Paris saw to it that these favourable statistics were kept out of the official record.

Quin's noble friends continued to back him, however. They

ensured that official note was taken of the homoeopaths' success. And when the Medical Registration Bill was introduced in 1858, Quin and his allies managed to have a clause included which forbade the medical schools from discriminating against students who wanted to practice homoeopathy.

By the time Quin died in 1878 there were about 300 homoeopathic doctors in Britain. Despite the noble patronage homoeopathic medicine did not thrive as a viable alternative to conventional medicine, however. Young doctors were schooled in orthodox techniques and could see no rhyme or reason in Hahnemann's ideas; most of them felt no inclination to put themselves out on a limb by trying them. Homoeopathic hospitals were established in Glasgow, Liverpool, Bristol and Tunbridge Wells as well as in London, but they were few among the many allopathic institutions. Patients who wanted homoeopathic treatment were usually faced with long journeys to reach their nearest homoeopathic specialist.

Homoeopathy was brought to the United States in the 1820s by a Danish doctor called Hans Gram and quickly became popular. As in England it was reported to be much more successful than allopathy in treating epidemic diseases, notably yellow fever which was a scourge of the Southern states. But over the years rifts opened in the ranks of the homoeopaths. Some followed the teachings of Tyler Kent, who was styled an 'ultra Hahnemannian' for his dogged pursuit of the founder's idea that patients were best treated by a microdose of the single substance best suited to their individual metabolism. Others, however, took the easier path of compromise and began to mix homoeopathy with conventional techniques. They were frankly scared of relying on homoeopathy for treating acute serious illnesses and argued that Hahnemann himself had not totally abandoned allopathic medicines for dealing with cases which needed urgent intervention. The disarray of the homoeopaths made them fall an easy victim to the American Medical Association which began imposing uniform educational standards on medical schools throughout the USA early this century.

Those doctors who were not overtly hostile to homoeopathy still argued that it would not do students any harm to learn conventional medical wisdom before embarking on homoeopathy. Far-sighted homoeopaths realized that this was the thin end of the wedge and that students would be indoctrinated against their teachings before they ever got the chance to test them for themselves. But like their British colleagues, the American homoeopaths thought it would be better to be included within the ambit of orthodox medicine rather than left outside like the osteopaths and chiropractors. After all they were doctors, not quacks. So what had they to fear from strengthening the bond with the allopaths?

Whether or not it was a political mistake to throw in their lot with the AMA is hard to say. If they had not joined up with orthodoxy, their decline might have been swifter. But it certainly did prove to be the thin end of the wedge. Their hospitals gradually adopted more allopathic techniques, they filled their empty beds with patients who wanted allopathic treatment, and recruited allopaths to treat them. Like osteopathy, homoeopathy degenerated into a mongrel practice with few practitioners who had the faith to stick to Hahnemann's principles alone.

One country where homoeopathy flourished and has continued to flourish is France. Although the French medical profession is most intolerant of laymen who practice unorthodox techniques like homoeopathy, osteopathy and acupuncture, it has been more than averagely inclined to try them itself.

There are ten times as many doctors practising homoeopathy in France than there are in Britain. Any tourist can get an idea of this interest when looking in a French pharmacist's window. Advertisements for homoeopathic remedies, often showing flowers or herbs in healthy bloom, can equal or outnumber those for allopathic medicines. The French homoeopathic faculty which trains doctors is a vigorous body which has continued to pursue research and provings of potential new remedies when their colleagues in Britain and America were clinging on for dear life.

India is the other main home of homoeopathy. Although most Indian doctors are trained in Western medicine, there are still many colleges where traditional forms of medicine are taught. And in these schools the philosophy of homoeopathy does not run against the conventional grain. Medicine is assumed to have a spiritual base, and a remedy is not looked at askance just because it does not have any material substance.

In Britain medicines without material substance, and the practitioners who prescribe them, get some very old-fashioned looks. A remarkable demonstration of the conventional attitude towards homoeopathy was given by a group of consultant physicians in Liverpool in March 1977. The consultants had met to decide amongst other things how they would share out facilities at the new Royal Liverpool Hospital. When it is finally completed the Royal Liverpool will be a veritable temple of medical technology, having cost over £60 million and taken 12 years to build.

Among the doctors at that meeting was Dr Geoffrey Martin, the city's only consultant homoeopath. Dr Martin had already witnessed the closure of the Liverpool Hahnemann Hospital the previous year. The hospital had been small, and the demand from patients for homoeopathic in-patient facilities had not been great enough to warrant the financially hard-pressed area health authority keeping it open. Reluctantly, Dr Martin had been forced to agree to treat his in-patients at the Mossley Hill Hospital, far from the city centre, and hold his out-patient sessions at the Liverpool Clinic. Nevertheless, he had been given to understand that when the new hospital was built, accommodation would be found for a proper Department of Homoeopathic Medicine.

In 1946 when the National Health Service was being planned, the then Minister of Health, Aneurin Bevan, had given 'an absolute guarantee' that homoeopathy would be allowed to continue within the new service and that it would remain available as long as there were doctors who wanted to practice it and patients who wanted to receive it.

When the matter of accommodation for the department of homoeopathy came up on the agenda of the meeting, Dr Martin was asked to leave the room – a request to which, surprisingly enough, he acceded. When Dr Martin was out of the room, the doctors discussed the proposed homoeopathic facilities and recorded the following 'unanimous' decision in the minutes:

The Division was horrified to learn that a Homoeopathy Clinic was suggested for the Royal Liverpool Hospital. They understand that this arose because of the takeover of the Hahnemann Hospital. However since beds for homoeopathy were provided at Mossley Hill Hospital, out-patient accommodation including the necessary pharmacy should be provided there.

They insisted unanimously that undergraduates should not be exposed to any unorthodox medicine before qualification, that the very existence of such a clinic in the hospital's prospectus would cause alarm to many doctors and patients, and that the Pharmacy should not be asked to attempt to supply expensive and unusual remedies.

Finally, they knew that under no circumstances would the Departments of Medicine or Clinical Pharmalogy allow any undergraduates to attend any such clinic and would not accept a Homoeopathist as a teaching hospital professional colleague. (Minute No 236 of the March, 1977 meeting of the Medicine Division of the Liverpool Area Health Authority, Central/Southern District).

To anyone with the least knowledge of homoeopathy it is clear that the doctors had got their facts a bit wrong. Apart from the fact that a decision can hardly be 'unanimous' when the only representative of one side of the argument is out of the room, it was rather mean of them to disparage Dr Martin so. He was a consultant physician with 25 years of unimpeachable experience. Even if they did not think much of him, they should have known that the Royal College of Physicians held a very good view of his abilities: shortly after this meeting he was elected a Fellow of the College, an honour which is not often granted to quacks or fools.

They were also wrong in suggesting that homoeopathic remedies were unusual and expensive. The average cost of commonly prescribed preparations is less than 50 pence for 200 pills, which compares very well with unbranded aspirin. Nor are they particularly unusual; specialist chemists can provide the whole range of homoeopathic medicines with minimum fuss.

But the doctors really gave themselves away by the emotive wording of their minute. As Tom Ellis, the Labour MP for Wrexham, commented when he brought the subject up in an adjournment debate in the House of Commons on 7 April 1977:

> For sheer blind prejudice and bigotry, crass ignorance and highly questionable ethical behaviour, it would be hard to find a better example, even from the minutes of the Wapping Bargees' Mutual Benefit Society, let alone a body of professional men.

Nevertheless, prejudice against homoeopathy is based on the belief that it is unscientific, that the evidence for its efficacy is anecdotal and that it has not been subjected to the rigours of contemporary scientific evaluation. Sadly, senior British homoeopaths have not bothered to answer this criticism as well as they might. Indeed, consultants at the Royal Homoeopathic Hospital in London have been outspoken in their antipathy to conducting clinical trials of homoeopathy which would have it objectively compared with orthodox forms of treatment. Some argue that the effect of homoeopathy cannot be measured like the effect of a drug because it is treating a whole person rather than a disease. Others are content to be empirical: it has worked for them, so there is no point trying to prove that it works to others. All this gives much comfort to the enemies of homoeopathy, who deduce that the homoeopaths have something – or should we say nothing – to hide.

Homoeopathic doctors in Glasgow have been more outward

looking. Early in 1978 Dr Robin Gibson and Dr Alistair MacNeill at the Glasgow Homoeopathic Hospital completed a year-long clinical trial involving 96 patients with rheumatoid arthritis. This disease is a chronic complaint which does not often respond well to treatment of any kind. The first drug usually prescribed by rheumatologists is aspirin, which is basically similar and a great deal less expensive than the more sophisticated anti-inflammatory drugs. Gibson, MacNeill and allopathic colleagues set about comparing the effects of homoeopathy against those of aspirin.

Half the patients were allocated to the homoeopaths. They were allowed to keep taking the anti-inflammatory drugs which they had been prescribed previously but were also given a homoeopathic remedy best suited to their individual constitution. The other half of the patients were treated by the allopathic rheumatologist with the standard large doses of aspirin used in the treatment of rheumatoid arthritis.

It would take another three books of this size to detail the reasons why particular remedies were chosen for particular patients in this trial. During the course of that year the 48 patients receiving homoeopathy were prescribed 150 different remedies between them. Subtle changes in the patient's condition might warrant the use of another remedy which would be better suited to their current feelings and symptoms. Sometimes a patient would reveal facts about his or her past life which had not been disclosed the first time the doctor took the medical history. Revelations about unhappy events during childhood or personal antagonism against friends and members of the family might, in the homoeopath's opinion, call for a fresh therapeutic approach.

Feelings and dietary likes and dislikes are not usually regarded as particularly significant symptoms by the conventional doctor treating arthritis. But the homoeopath regards them as very important; remember that he is not trying to select the right drug for the disease but the right drug for the patient, regardless of the disease. A normal clinical trial tests a drug, but Gibson and MacNeill's trial was testing much more. It was testing their ability to use a wide range of remedies on a wide variety of patients. It was the doctors as much as the drugs who were on trial.

By the end of the year less than 15 per cent of the aspirin patients were still in the game. They had found the drug unsatisfactory and been put on alternative medication. In the homoeopathy group, however, 42 per cent of the patients had been able to give up all drugs and another 30 per cent had reduced their drug intake and were able to move more freely than before.

Sceptics often suggest that homoeopathy is 'placebo' medicine. A placebo is an inert substance, a dummy pill or tonic, which looks and tastes like the real thing. Some patients respond very well to placebos, but the good effects usually wear off after a few weeks. At the same time as Drs Gibson and MacNeill were doing their trial, another Glasgow rheumatologist was comparing the effects of a placebo and a new anti-inflammatory drug on another 100 patients with rheumatoid arthritis. He found that after three weeks 30 per cent of his placebo patients were still happy with what they were getting. But at the end of six weeks they had all complained that the treatment was no longer working.

It is unusual in clinical trials to let the patients continue with their previous medication while they begin a new course of treatment. Nevertheless, the trial, which was written up in the *Journal of Clinical Pharmacology* (due for publication later in 1978), did show that homoeopathy was considerably better than placebos and very probably a lot better than aspirin. Not a resounding victory perhaps, but a start in the right direction.

An important element of homoeopathy is the doctor himself. A great deal depends on his ability to draw out the patient's character and symptoms and find the corresponding remedy. And because he is paying a great deal more attention to the patient than the conventional doctor might, the patient may feel much better, whether or not the remedy is having an effect.

To sort out how much the treatment's success can be attributed to the doctor and how much to the therapy, Dr Gibson and his colleagues are conducting another long trial which had only reached the half-way stage when this book went to press. This time all the patients will be given aspirin. Half of them will get a placebo as well as their aspirin, the other half will get a homoeopathic remedy. If the success of homoeopathy does just boil down to the attention the doctor gives the patient, then all of them should respond equally well. To establish how much of its success depends on the diagnostic skill of the individual doctor, the patients will be shared between two homoeopaths. If individual skill is not significant, both doctors' patients should respond equally well, or badly. If one doctor is much better than the other at choosing the correct remedy from the vast homoeopathic pharmacopia, his group should come off best.

You can get an idea of the complexity of homoeopathic diagnosis by looking at the profusion of remedies available to the homoeopath for treating the common cold. An allopathic doctor regards colds as pretty much of a muchness and will usually suggest a general symptomatic treatment like aspirin, bed rest and hot drinks. For the homoeopath there are many kinds of cold, each of which calls for a different remedy. A patient who complains of constant sneezing, watery eyes, headache, cough, hoarseness and a nose which is runny with a very acrid discharge, and who feels better when he is in a cold room than in a warm room, would be prescribed the remedy *Allium cepa*, which is derived from red onions. A patient who felt permanently thirsty, anxious and restless, had burning sensations in the nose and eyes, fever, headache and insomnia but felt better in a warm room might get *Arsenicum album*, a potentization of arsenic trioxide. Matching the symptoms to the remedy is crucial; and the correct remedy is the one which in larger doses could produce similar side effects in a healthy prover.

Proving possible remedies is a delicate, time-consuming business and has not been pursued very actively in Britain and the United States in recent years, though Dr Trevor Smith, a psychiatrist who recently became interested in homoeopathy, is embarking on some new provings in London.

First, of course, you have to get hold of healthy volunteers, which is not easy. Then over a period of weeks they have to note down every reaction which might have been brought on by the substance they are proving.

Effects which are reported by all or nearly all the volunteers are recorded in the homoeopathic *Materia Medica* as 'characteristics'. Frequently reported effects which crop up in some but not in others are categorized as 'generals'. Effects which come and go, which might be aggravated by cold air but eased by warmth for instance, are entered as 'modalities'. When it comes to prescribing, unless the doctor is experienced he can spend hours riffling through the cross references of the *Materia Medica* before he finds a remedy to fit the patient accurately.

Although homoeopathy is based on the principle of 'like cures like', its practitioners have only a vague idea of why this should be so. Quinine is not the only substance which conventional medicine acknowledges to have the effect of producing similar symptoms to the disease it fights. Iodine can temporarily relieve the disease toxic goitre, which is caused by an overactive thyroid gland producing too much iodine. Why iodine should help the body stop producing iodine is a puzzle.

Dr Robin Gibson suggests that disease is the result of an inability to deal effectively with a particular element; this inability would affect complex enzyme processes in the body.

There is good evidence that the body contains traces of every element in the earth, and quite possibly in the same proportion as they exist in nature. The body needs these elements, but if the receptors or enzymes which use these elements are not functioning properly, you might get a toxic reaction. In some types of 'flu the patient may experience all the symptoms of mild arsenic poisoning – anxiety, restlessness, burning sensations. The homoeopathic remedy made from arsenic corrects the defect.

To describe a homoeopathic remedy as 'like curing like' gives only half of the picture, though. When Hahnemann experimented with small doses, he did not stop at dilutions of one in ten or one in a hundred. His method – which is still followed today – consisted of taking one measure of the basic herbal tincture or chemical and shaking it vigorously with nine measures of water and/or alcohol. If the material was not soluble it would be ground up with lactose (milk sugar). That gave a dilution or 'potency' of 1x. If that solution was then taken and shaken with another nine parts of the base, the resulting potency was called 2x. He was soon using potencies of 12x, which is one part in a billion. He then went on to shaking (the homoeopaths call it 'succussing') one part of the tincture with a hundred parts of water. That gave him the first centisimal potency, called 1C for short. Modern homoeopathy uses potencies of up to 200C. By this stage there is only the tiniest chance that even one molecule of the original diluted substance is left. Less than a drop in the ocean. If homoeopathic remedies really do work at such potencies, it is no longer a matter of 'like curing like' but rather 'what was once like curing like'. Conventional doctors who can accept that the herbal base of a remedy might have beneficial effects just give up hope at this point.

Before you too abandon yourself to despair, I would draw your attention to a report which appeared in the *Daily Telegraph*, on 19 August 1954:

RESEARCH REVEALS NEW FORCE IN PHYSICS

Latent Energy Found In Drugs After Dilution

The existence of a new force in physics has been demonstrated scientifically after research lasting 15 years. It is new to medicine and to science as a whole. It has been shown, says a report published today, that a drug diluted almost to infinity, so that not one molecule of the original drug remains in the solution, retains a form of energy which will affect living cells. The power of the solution does not depend solely on the degree of dilution but on a special progressive method in its preparation. The energy latent in the drug is apparently liberated and increased by a forceful shaking of the liquid at each stage of the process.

The unidentified force is now being investigated. 'It seems that it goes beyond the material,' one who has followed the experiments closely explained to me. 'We have reached the outside edge of what the world knows scientifically.'

The scientist who had so boldly trod to the edge of the known scientific world was the Glasgow physician Professor W. E. Boyd. Boyd was himself a homoeopath, but he was not content with the traditional empirical approach to the speciality. He argued that if microdoses worked in humans, then it should be possible to make them work in the test tube too.

The report in the *Daily Telegraph* referred to a series of experiments Boyd had conducted at his laboratory in 1946, 1948 and 1952, which were written up in the *British Journal of Homoeopathic* in April 1954. His tests were designed to establish whether microdose solutions of mercuric chloride, which is used as a homoeopathic remedy, could cause biochemical or biological activity.

The most straightforward way of demonstrating this in the laboratory was to measure the rate at which starch was hydrolized, or broken down, by the enzyme diastase. For his tests, and he performed 500 of them between 1946 and 1952, he took flasks containing distilled water, diastase and soluble starch and similar flasks containing diastase, soluble starch and microdoses of mercuric chloroid. The microdoses, which had been prepared by standard mechanical succussion techniques used by homoeopathic chemists, were 30C potencies, in other words dilutions of 10^{-61}, in which, theoretically at least, not one molecule of the original mercuric chloride could be present. The enzyme activity was then studied with the help of an instrument called the Spekker absorptionmeter, an early form of spectograph, and the results were subjected to independent statistical analysis. Analysis of those 500 experiments showed that the microdosed solution had a highly significant effect on the breakdown of the starch.

Boyd's experiments were designed to find out *whether* the

microdose had any effect, not *how* it might work. The main problem was to ensure that the dilutions really were as weak as the homoeopaths claimed. Sceptics still point out that the glass flasks used for succussing solutions are quite absorbent and that unless great care is taken cleaning them out after each operation, significant amounts of the original tincture – or indeed other substances like washing-up liquid – could adhere to the sides of the flask and spoil the purity of the next solution poured into it. To forestall criticisms of this kind Boyd had had his bottle washing methods checked and approved by the Isotope School at Harwell, the nuclear research station.

In fact, all the possible hazards which could have led to mistakes had been taken into account when preparing the experiments. For once a serious scientist had come up with evidence that the microdose did have a measureable effect. The paper he presented was over 40 pages long and could not be faulted. The only snag was that when Boyd repeated the experiments some years later with the same lab technician he had worked with before, he was unable to get similar positive results.

Investigations of homoeopathy have been fraught with such tribulations. Dr Victor Moss, a research scientist at the Institute of Physiology at Glasgow University, has recently done a series of experiments to test whether homoeopathic remedies used for treating infections have any measurable effect on leucocytes, the white blood cells which fight infection. His laboratory experiments have shown that the effects are more than you would get by chance; nevertheless, they are very variable.

In France, Professor Netien and his colleagues at the University of Lyons showed by experiment in 1970 that plants which had been poisoned by copper sulphate could be revived by giving them an attenuated dose of the same substance. Dr Moss has tried similar experiments himself, using fresh-water algae, but could not get the same results. Some batches of a 15C potency of copper sulphate did stimulate the growth rate of poisoned algae, but the same effect was noticed in the unpoisoned algae too. If the microdose had had the effect a homoeopath would expect it to have, it would have stimulated the poisoned algae but done nothing to the normal algae.

The work of Boyd, Netien and Moss is just a sample of the laboratory research made of homoeopathy. In the United States Dr James Stephenson has also investigated the effect of microdilutions in the test tube and has come up with positive results. But almost all the persistent investigators have come up against the bugbear of unrepeatability.

Dr Victor Moss points out that most of the published papers have barely got beyond the status of 'preliminary communications'. In many the researcher's method can be faulted. And the problem with many of the older experiments is that, even if you wanted to repeat them, it would be difficult to ascertain exactly what the original researcher actually did. As Dr Moss says, 'Some are mumbo-jumbo. But there is a hard core of experiments which seem hard to fault. They ought to be repeated. But usually if they are repeated the results are different – not necessarily negative, but different.'

If the microdose does work, how are we to explain this 'new force in physics'?

In 1949 the physicist P. W. Bridgman published a book called *Physics at High Pressure*, which pointed out that water which was frozen under a pressure of six atmospheres crystallized quite differently from water frozen at normal pressure. If that same water were thawed and then refrozen at one atmosphere it would crystallize as it had done under high pressure.

This led to the notion that water could hold a 'message' or pattern and that such patterns might be imprinted in water subjected to the homoeopathic succussion technique.

This idea was taken up by Dr G. O. Barnard of the National Physical Laboratory. In 1965 he pointed out that water molecules had been observed under certain conditions to form long chains, or polymers. These polymers could apparently be formed, and broken, by vigorous vibration. This, he suggested, could be the result of ionization, charging the water with positive ions. When a substance was dissolved in water, the water molecules had to make way for the intruding molecules, and in so doing they formed a configuration corresponding to the shape of the molecules of the dissolved substance – rather like a mould.

Barnard then postulated that this 'moulded' water created polymers in the same configuration when it was itself diluted and succussed with untreated water. In other words, dilution and succussion was creating a kind of negative image or ghost of the dissolved substance. 'What Hahnemann found quite by accident was a means of separating the structural informational content of a chemical from its associated chemical mass,' he wrote.

Barnard's ideas did not receive rapturous applause from the scientific establishment and he too died before he could complete a satisfactory series of experiments to back his theory. Homoeopaths who feel the need for a theory now suggest that succussion of a remedy releases the energy of the substance from its mass and speculate that an explanation for their form of medicine may be found in quantum physics.

However large the theoretical loopholes in homoeopathy may be, and despite the lack of interest shown by most doctors, homoeopathy is making a gradual come-back. For the past five years the number of new patients at the London Homoeopathic Hospital has been rising by ten per cent a year. For the most part these are patients who have not been well served by orthodox medicine. Courses for doctors organized by the Faculty of Homoeopathy are oversubscribed, even though they are not recognized by the Postgraduate Medical Federation and receive no official assistance or funding.

Even most devoted homoeopathic consultants like Robin Gibson do not claim that homoeopathy is a complete system of medicine. But they do claim great success in treating chronic disease, allergies, children's diseases and infections. It could be a valuable tool for all doctors, but as yet the medical profession as a whole is not convinced. If homoeopathy is to survive in a hostile economic and professional climate, it will have to prove its worth, and its practitioners show that they are not afraid to let their effectiveness be measured against that of their allopathic colleagues.

4 Herbalism—The Grass is Greener

In November 1976 the Royal College of Physicians held a conference in London to discuss how the medical profession and the pharmaceutical industry could deal with an unpleasant scientific, ethical and political problem. The conference had been called in the aftermath of the frightening discovery that a heart drug, practolol, could cause severe eye damage, sometimes even blindness, in some of the patients who had been prescribed it.

ICI, the manufacturers of practolol, had scrupulously tested the drug according to all the prevailing rules and criteria before they were allowed to launch it on the market. It was a very effective drug and quickly proved popular with doctors, and with patients suffering from angina and high blood pressure. It was not until several months later that a doctor at Moorfields Eye Hospital realized that the only common factor in a number of patients who had been referred to him with an unusual eye complaint was that they were all on practolol. By this time tens of thousands of patients throughout the country were being prescribed the drug.

The doctor reported his alarming findings to the Committee on the Safety of Medicines, which duly issued a 'yellow peril' warning to all doctors telling them of the potential hazard. This warning prompted a flurry of correspondence to the Committee from doctors whose patients were suffering similar side-effects. Very few of these doctors had apparently associated their patients' complaint of 'dry eyes' with the drug until the connection was drawn to their attention. As the side-effects seriously afflicted only a minority of patients, a GP with fifty or a hundred patients on practolol might still not have noticed anything amiss. The question posed at the Royal

College of Physicians' meeting was 'how do we deal with unforeseen side-effects of drugs, and who should bear ultimate responsibility for the damage they cause?'

As far as the law is concerned, an individual doctor can be held liable for damage done to a patient in the course of treatment, however unwittingly. That is of course a bit hard on the doctors who might assume that a drug produced by a major manufacturer and which has come up to the standards demanded by the Committee on the Safety of Medicines was a safe bet. And what about the patient's responsibility? Is it reasonable for them to expect that medical treatment should be guaranteed risk-free? At the turn of the century when medical science was not held in such awe as it is today, it was taken for granted that anyone who fell into the clutches of the medical profession, especially of surgeons, would very likely not survive the encounter.

Sir Eric Scowen, chairman of the Committee on the Safety of Medicines, exonerated the government by pointing out that the CSM did not *approve* new drugs. It simply *allowed* them to be introduced once they had met reasonable standards of safety, quality and efficacy. When this book went to press his Committee was still discussing ways of restricting distribution of new drugs to a small number of doctors who would confine their prescribing to a few thousand patients. If no adverse effects had cropped up after some months, the drug could then be released to the whole medical profession.

ICI, who did not want to undergo the trial by newspaper suffered by the Distillers Company, manufacturers of thalidomide, decided to offer compensation to patients who could prove they had been damaged by practolol. They did insist, however, that they were not legally obliged to do so.

Dr D. G. Davey, who had been research director of ICI Pharmaceuticals when practolol was launched, pointed out that 10,000 chemical compounds might be synthesized before one with suitable medicinal properties was found. Safety testing of potential medicines included prolonged tests for toxicity, their effects on reproduction and their likelihood of inducing cancer. Metabolic investigations first had to be done in rats and dogs, and finally in human volunteers. The whole business could take up to five years.

Drugs, he suggested, are among the purests substances we have. 'If a cabbage were subjected to spectroscopic analysis and presented to the Committee on the Safety of Medicines, it would be rejected outright.'

Cabbage does of course have side-effects, though they are anti-social rather than physically dangerous. But Dr Davey's comment reflects how pharmaceutical science has turned full circle during the past century. Before the German drug industry got into full swing around 1880, very nearly all the medicines available to doctors were plant-based. Many drugs are still derived from plants, but the industry has concentrated on isolating their most active ingredients. Whenever possible these active ingredients have been chemically analysed and replaced by a synthetic substitute which can be made in a factory.

Herbal medicine has been practised as long as man has existed. Ironically, just at the moment when we had enough science to be able to investigate herbs thoroughly, the medical profession opted for chemicals instead. For the late-nineteenth-century industrial pharmacist, herbs were a mess. Chemically they are a highly elaborate complex of proteins, enzymes, phenols, vitamins, terpenoids, inorganic salts, polycelluloses, glycosides, chlorophyll and trace elements. Many of the chemicals in plants had not been 'discovered' and labelled by contemporary science. Not only that, herbalism was notoriously tied up with superstition and magic. So it seemed much more scientific and rational to look for substances which had a measurable effect, which could be purified and prescribed in neat, packageable doses.

It is only recently that we have seen that these qualities do not necessarily offer the panacea. What price purity, if it sends you blind?

When the pharmaceutical industry does alight on a herb of therapeutic value, the results are not always beneficial. Rauwolfia, the snakeroot, has been used for centuries in India as a sedative and cure for high blood pressure. Mahatma

Gandhi used to drink snakeroot tea every night before he went to bed. In the 1950s an Indian medical research team isolated the plant's most potent alkaloid, reserpine. Purified, carefully measured doses of reserpine worked marvellously as an anti-hypertensive. But in less than 20 years the drug has gone out of fashion because it can cause severe depression, Parkinsonism and a host of milder but unpleasant side-effects.

Herbalists point out that in its natural state rauwolfia contains an assortment of salts, trace elements and proteins which made it a great deal easier for the body to assimilate than the single purified alkaloid.

This may be true. It is well known that when otherwise inert or only mildly active chemicals are put together, they can exert an effect much greater than they can achieve individually. This phenomenon is called synergism. It is also possible that some substances in rauwolfia could counteract the excesses of the single alkaloid and act as a kind of braking mechanism.

The trouble with these appealing explanations is that no one knows for certain whether they are true of all herbs. Modern Western drugs are monitored for side-effects for years after their introduction. Such intense scrutiny has not been applied to many herbal medicines.

Digitalis offers an example of the benefits which can accrue from serious investigation of a herbal remedy. In 1775 William Withering, a physician of Birmingham, was shown a recipe containing a score of herbs which a 'wise woman' in Shropshire had been giving villagers as a cure for the dropsy – what we now call oedema or water retention. The remedy was remarkably effective, and Withering set about trying to find its secret. He finally identified its most significant ingredient as the root of the foxglove, *digitalis*, and he decided to use the plant in his own practice. But experiment found that the leaves of the foxglove were more potent than the root, especially if they were gathered while the flower was in bloom.

Even today doctors find it difficult to prescribe digitalis correctly without overdosing the patient and bringing out a variety of side-effects. These side-effects include vomiting, loss of appetite, giddiness, cold sweats, a very slow pulse, and, in extreme overdosage, convulsions and death.

Withering kept a detailed catalogue of the benefits and adverse reactions of his foxglove preparations. The old Shropshire wise woman had claimed that her remedy cured dropsy by making the patient vomit. Withering realized that she must have been giving them a massive overdose. He noticed that the drug had a cumulative effect. It was retained by the body, so if it was taken regularly its effects became ever greater. It cured dropsy, sure enough, but unless dosage was strictly controlled, it could give patients even worse complaints.

Withering's paper *An Account of the Foxglove* was a medical landmark. He set the style for subsequent pharmacological investigation by meticulously observing and recording the medicine's effects on a large number of patients. And by applying a scientific mind to a remedy which most of his medical contemporaries would have decried as a dangerous quack nostrum, he discovered a substance which is still used in medicine today.

We now know that digitalis acts on the heart, slowing its beat and making each contraction of the heart muscle stronger. Dropsy develops when a weak heart cannot keep blood flushing through the system strongly enough to stop fluid accumulating in the surrounding tissue. Once the heart is stimulated by the drug, the improvement in circulation helps the kidneys work more efficiently, and the surplus fluids are filtered away to the bladder.

The fact that Withering did not know that digitalis acted on the heart is irrelevant. He opened the door to further investigation. Unfortunately the investigative methods he pioneered 200 years ago have not been widely applied to herbal medicines since. We have a great deal of knowledge about the side-effects of chemical drugs, and this has made many people think they should be avoided. Herbs have not suffered from bad publicity, and it is fashionably assumed that because they are 'natural' they are safe.

Many of the chemicals which pollute our air and seas can

cause cancer. But one of the most potent known carcinogens is a natural substance produced by fungi which grow on soya beans. Most herbs which are powerful medicines are equally powerful poisons when taken in excessive doses. Digitalis is one example. Parsley can cause haemorrhage. Camomile and yarrow can cause vertigo and nausea. Sage can cause abortions – if taken in massive doses. Before we abandon chemicals in favour of herbs we should remember Sir Derrick Dunlop's adage: 'Show me a medicine without adverse effects, and I will show you a useless medicine.'

'Herb' is a portmanteau definition which covers all plants valued for their scent, flavour, colour or as foods and medicines. Of the 350,000 known and named species of plant, only 10,000 have been investigated for their medicinal properties. Of these 10,000 about 200 are used by British herbalists. In North America native herbalists have identified about 450 species which they use as medicine.

Herbal medicine was invented by animals. Anyone who has had a dog or cat as a pet must have noticed how the creature seeks out certain plants when it feels sick. Mint is popular with flatulent cats and is prescribed by herbalists as a digestive. (The After Eight mint chocolates which are palated by would-be sophisticates are the degenerate descendant of an effective herbal medicine. Try offering your cat an After Eight and a leaf of mint. If he has not been totally corrupted by human ways, he will go for the latter.)

It did not take long for men and animals to work out that some plant foods tended to block the gut while others gave them the runs. The earliest form of bandage was a leaf, and people noticed that some leaves seemed to speed healing and relieve pain better than others. Over the years a body of knowledge was built up.

The inquisitive souls in ancient times who studied herbs had no conception of the science we call chemistry. The notion that matter could be subdivided into thousands of different substances would have been quite alien to their way of thought. In most ancient cultures the world was regarded as an interaction between four elements, fire, air, earth and water, with a breath of divine intervention to get the whole thing going.

Without chemistry to explain how one substance could act on another, they had to fall back on other sciences. The favourite was astrology. The various powers of plants were ascribed to the movements of the heavenly bodies, and complex correlations were drawn between the position of planets and the time plants sprouted or came into bloom.

Paracelsus and Nicholas Culpeper, the most famous of British herbalists, made much of the supposed affinities between herbs and the stars. Culpeper is much reviled by modern herbalists, who are keen to banish what they regard as the mumbo-jumbo of astrology from their craft. They point out that Culpeper drew nearly all his knowledge of herbs from John Gerarde and John Parkinson, who published their great Herbals in 1597 and 1636 respectively. Astrology, the moderns suggest, was just an obscurantist addendum to the straightforward, practical observations on which true herbalism had been based.

Oddly enough, some of the few doctors who have an abiding interest in herbalism are more inclined to accept the astrological aspect of herbalism than the lay herbalists. These doctors, most of them homoeopaths, follow the teachings of Rudolf Steiner, the Austrian mystic-cum-scientist. Steiner held that health was a dynamic equilibrium between man and all the forces of the universe. The planets, the Sun and the Moon were among the most powerful of these forces. Steiner made correlations between minerals, plants, the planets and the various organs of the body, and based much of his medical therapies on them.

He also regarded man himself as an interplay between three forces. There was his 'thinking' aspect, associated with the brain, nerves and sensory organs, which controlled intellect. The second aspect, 'feeling', centred on the lungs, heart and blood vessels. This was concerned with spreading energies around the body, and thus with emotion. The third aspect he called 'will', but it might better be described as instinct or gut reaction. It was concerned with reproduction, movement and metabolism, and centred on the abdomen which houses the vital organs which perform these processes.

Plants, according to Steiner, have a similar three-part structure, but with them it is the other way up. The roots correspond to the brain and do the plant's hunting and gathering. The leaves and stems are responsible for the flow of sap and salts. The flowers and fruit are concerned with reproduction and are also most strongly influenced by the pull of environmental and cosmic forces.

Steiner recommended that herbal remedies should be based on that part of the plant which corresponded to the disturbed aspect of the patient. Migraine, for instance would, be treated with a root, a heart complaint with leaf.

Steiner's teachings, which are the basis of the Anthroposophy movement, covered very much more than the ideas just outlined. He presented an all-embracing philosophy-cum-science-cum-religion which proclaimed that physical matter was formed and activated by cosmic forces.

His idea that parts of a plant correspond with parts of the human make-up echoes another old herbalist belief. The greatest powers have always been attached to plants which have a similar shape to the human body. The mandrake, or mandragora, and ginseng have been vaunted as panaceas largely because of their humanoid form. Other plants have been ascribed properties due to their particular characteristics. St John's wort, for example, has leaves which look as though they have been pricked by hundreds of pins. It was worn as a talisman to protect the bearer from sharp objects like swords, and bolts of lightning. Mistletoe, found on apple, and the rowan (from which, according to legend, the Cross was made), symbolized man's power over nature. Salad burnett, with its flowers the colour of dried blood, was reckoned to be good for staunching wounds.

The medieval alchemist regarded dew as the purest distillation of the element water. Any plant which seemed to attract or retain dew was held in special awe. Lady's Mantle, whose scientific name is *Alchemilla vulgaris*, closed its petals at night. They would open in the morning filled with dew.

The fact that it had nine petals – nine being a magical number – increased its reputation.

The sundew is a carnivorous plant which grows on poor soil and sustains itself by trapping small insects with a sticky liquid it exudes. Old herbalists regard this liquid as a dew, and because this 'dew' never evaporated, it was thought to be a recipe for eternal youth.

This history of astrology and sympathetic magic is an embarrassment to the majority of modern herbalists: 'You won't find us creeping out at full moon or swinging pendulums over our plants,' says John Hyde, a partner in the Leicester herbal clinic which is the biggest enterprise of its kind in Europe. He is also the public relations man for the National Institute of Medical Herbalists, which campaigns as best it can for higher standards in the craft.

For the NIMH higher standards must be based on sound knowledge of chemistry, pharmacology, anatomy, physiology, pathology and medical law. The Institute runs a four-year part-time course of study, at the end of which successful students are awarded its diploma. Astrology and radiesthesia are not on the curriculum. A few of the Institute's 100 members may use these techniques in their own practice, but it is not the policy of the NIMH to let this be widely known.

John Hyde's consulting room is very much like that of a general medical practitioner. He uses a stethoscope, blood pressure gauge, and other diagnostic tools. The dispensary is run by ladies in white coats, and the waiting-room is well provided with old magazines.

Herbalists do not attempt to diagnose disease in the way a doctor would. Like the homoeopaths they are more interested in the symptoms and the person, and their treatment is aimed at relieving symptoms and stimulating the system as a whole. By adopting this approach they have also avoided making themselves appear to be in direct competition with the medical profession. Herbal prescribing is a mixture of art and science. Prescriptions may contain upwards of a dozen different tinctures, some aimed at relieving the symptoms and others as a general tonic. 'The word "anti-biotic" literally means anti-life,' John Hyde declared. 'We would treat many infections with yellow dock, *rumex crispus*, which increases the white blood cells rather than attacking particular organisms. This way resistance to disease lasts long after the infection has passed.'

Some herbalists prescribe dried, chopped or powdered herbs to their patients. But most find that their remedies are not very palatable in this form, especially if the patient has to take more than a small mouthful. Instead, they make liquid extracts or tinctures by steeping the herbs in water or alcohol, which can then be prescribed as a liquid medicine or added to a base and made into pills.

Water and alcohol cannot extract all the active ingredients, however, and the leaf of the plant is sometimes used when it has greater medicinal value than a tincture. Chewing also subjects the leaf to very different chemical processes than it would go through if it were swallowed whole. Enzymes in the saliva of the mouth break down starches in the leaf, converting them to sugar more efficiently than if they were gulped down quickly.

The method of preparation can radically alter a herb's function. Fresh comfrey root, for example, is rich in edible fibre and mucilage and therefore a potent laxative. If it is added to alcohol, the mucilage is broken down, and the major remaining constituent is tannin, which binds the intestinal tract and is effective against diarrhoea.

Unlike other lay groups in Britain whose right to practise their particular therapies is protected by Common Law, herbalists have found themselves hedged around with regulations. Their freedom to practice was originally granted by a statute passed in the reign of Henry VIII, but now their activities are curtailed by twentieth-century laws aimed at restricting the availability of potentially harmful medicines.

Attempts have been made during the past hundred years to introduce compulsory registration and licensing for herbalists, but all the Bills failed. Anyone who sets up in practice as a herbalist is bound by the 1968 Medicines Act which sets standards to ensure that herbal remedies are prepared in hygienic surroundings and that they do not contain dangerous substances picked up from the air or soil where they were grown. (Some plants have a liking for certain poisonous elements. Thyme, for instance, takes up lead, and herbalists have to take care that their thyme was not grown in lead-bearing soil.)

The Medicines Commission, which oversees all aspects of medicines from production to prescription, has a sub-committee which deals specifically with herbal remedies and is supposed to examine them for evidence of undesirable side effects. Since 1965 the National Institute of Medical Herbalists has teamed up with doctors, pharmacists and pharmacognosists to produce a British Herbal Pharmacopoeia. When it is complete this should be a definitive reference book in several volumes, unique in the history of herbalism. Chemical analysis of the herbs described in the Pharmacopoeia is being made by pharmacognosists at London University's School of Pharmacy, and reports of their effects are provided by the more experienced practising members of the Institute.

Although herbalists like John Hyde protest that their work is strangled by regulations, the scientific and political interest which is beginning to be shown in herbalism should eventually benefit everyone. The Medicines Act of 1968 contains a clause which specifically allows the herbal practitioner to prescribe remedies to patients 'in accordance with his own judgement as to the treatment required'. No other group of non-medically qualified practitioners has been given similar legal recognition.

There is now a plethora of books on the market which extol the nutritive and medical virtues of herbs. Close examination will often reveal that they differ considerably in their recommendations as to how particular herbs should be used and even where they can be found. This chaos in the literature prompted the scientifically oriented Herb Society to launch an appeal for £500,000 in 1977 to pay for a thorough analysis of the data collected throughout the ages and throughout the world.

'There is still so much mythology attached to herbs,' a biologist working for the Herb Society explained. 'So much of the herbalists' knowledge has been handed down unquestioned from one generation to the next; names of plants have been mistranslated – especially in Europe – and sometimes their properties have been ascribed to completely different species. Our task is to sort the fact from the fiction.' However, the Herb Society's attempts to interest official bodies like the Medical Research Council in its project have met with little enthusiasm.

The wild claims of some herbalists have not endeared them to the circumspect scientific establishment. Ironically, the wildest claims sometimes obscure a plant's real value and discourage serious researchers from investigating it. A prime example is ginseng. This plant's scientific name is *panax*, meaning panacea, and it is alleged by its afficionados to be quite literally a cure-all. When someone proclaims that he has a cure-all for sale, sensible folk cry 'Quack'. Much has been made of the vaguely human shape of the ginseng root, and sceptics dismissed it as another exercise in sympathetic magic.

Nevertheless, pharmacologists who have studied the chemistry of ginseng have found that it contains, among other things, glycosides not found in any other plant. Glycosides are substances which help the body produce sugar, fight off infectious disease, and render unwanted chemicals inert. Although the ginseng glycosides are unique to the plant, they do have strong similarities with glycosides found in digitalis.

Ginseng has won glowing testimonials from military men. General Westmorland, the former American commander in Vietnam is reported to have been an enthusiast. Those who are not impressed by the recommendations of American generals may be interested to learn that Russian cosmonauts take ginseng in space.

Extracts from the periwinkle plant have produced four drugs, vinblastine, vincristine, vinleurosine and vinrosidine, which are effective against certain forms of cancer. Garlic too appears to have an ability to control tumours, as indeed do many hundreds of plants. The National Cancer Institute in the United States has checked over 1500 plant extracts for possible anti-cancer properties and found that more than 50 of them did inhibit the growth of tumours in laboratory mice.

While herbalists are delighted to see high-powered twentieth-century medical research teams credit their beloved plants with curative properties (some of which had been recognized centuries ago), they believe that much modern research is ignoring their real value. In the February 1977 issue of the medical journal *MIMS Magazine*, Fletcher Hyde, chairman of the British Herbal Pharmacopoeia Committee, suggested that the 'cardinal principle of herbal medicine is prescribing the whole plant'. He cited the dandelion as an example.

It is not for nothing that the dandelion is known in some places as *Wet the bed*. It is a strong diuretic and therefore very useful against dropsy. The drugs most commonly prescribed against water retention have the effect of depleting the body's potassium. This leads to constipation, loss of appetite, muscle weakness and can also interfere with the working of the heart. As a result patients on diuretics usually have to be given potassium supplements. Dandelion on the other hand has a high natural content of potassium. So the plant not only offers an effective treatment but also an inbuilt compensation against side-effects.

Three hundred thousand plants have been identified; there may be another half million as yet undiscovered. A tiny minority has been looked at for healing properties. At present herbalism is being kept going by a mere handful of devotees. Healing, homoeopathy and herbalism have superficially little in common. (Admittedly most homoeopathic remedies have a herbal base, but their method of preparation is quite different.) Nevertheless, the practitioners of all three techniques have a common approach; they claim to be dealing with the whole person rather than a disease. The healer, who is generally quite ignorant of pathology, channels some vital energy; the medical homoeopath knows how to diagnose disease in the conventional way but aims his treatment at the patient's whole constitution; and the herbalist, prescribing a multitude of medicines at once, is likewise trying to improve the whole body's defences rather than eliminate a particular destructive organism. Their approach is holistic. This may sound very well, but is it really more valid than the conventional approach? One of the principles of conventional medicine is that it is easier to identify and treat a disease than to prescribe health. The healers, homoeopaths and herbalists do aim at creating health. Seen this way their various techniques strike me as being complementary to conventional medicine rather than an alternative.

The holistic approach has not been completely ignored by doctors working in the mainstream of medicine. The next two chapters should show how thinking healthy can overcome the most savage kinds of disease.

5 Biofeedback—Self-Control in Croydon

Driving from where I live in West London to Croydon, that drear con-suburbation appended to the nether regions of the metropolis, is a task which the people who manufactured my motor car, the town planners who built the roads, and the good Lord who designed my body never intended me to perform. The journey is boring – with nothing more colourful than a red traffic light to gladden the eye – hazardous – with four major road works and twenty child-infested ice-cream vans at any given time or season – and unhealthy.

The only thing which could inspire a sane person to make that journey is money, and it was for this very reason that I made it. I had been commissioned by the BBC to do a radio feature on Dr Chandra Patel, a Croydon general practitioner, who was working on a new approach to the treatment of high blood pressure. By the time I had completed the hellish twenty-mile trip I had rendered myself a suitable candidate for her clinic.

High blood pressure, hypertension for short, is a puzzling disease. Sometimes it appears as a symptom of an underlying complaint, like kidney disease, and will go if that complaint can be cured. But its more common form, what is called essential hypertension, is harder to pin down. First of all, you may have high blood pressure and know nothing about it. Various mild symptoms such as dizziness and headaches have been associated with hypertension, but whether they are actually caused by it is hard to say.

You might think that a disease without symptoms is not a disease at all. That would be a rash conclusion, however. The life insurance companies, who study medical statistics with even more zeal than the medical profession itself, recognize that high blood pressure is a reliable indicator of a low life expectancy. Applicants who undergo an insurance medical and are found to be hypertensive will almost certainly be obliged to pay higher premiums.

Even so, no one is really certain what normal blood pressure is. The average blood pressure of Western Europeans is higher than that of Africans, and wide differences occur between apparently healthy individuals of the same race and culture. The average blood pressure in Western Europe may be well above what should be regarded as normal or healthy.

There is a growing body of medical opinion which believes that hypertension and many other complaints are caused by stress. Stress is still a controversial term in medicine, and it is only quite recently that most leading medical journals gave up insisting that the word should appear in inverted commas whenever it was written in a scientific paper.

Briefly, stress means anything which upsets the body's equilibrium and prevents it from functioning smoothly. Infectious, injuries and dietary deficiencies are all potential stressors, but most commonly it is emotional disorders which get the blame for causing the 'stress diseases'.

Emotional disorders may be too strong a term. 'Bad habits' would be more accurate. It is quite healthy, for instance, for your blood pressure to shoot up when someone with wild eyes rushes towards you brandishing a broken bottle. The unpleasant vision prompts the sympathetic nervous system to release adrenaline and noradrenaline which stimulate the heart, increase circulation in the muscles, halt the digestive processes, and get you ready to run. This is the 'fight or flight' mechanism at work, and a very useful mechanism it is if you want to survive in a world of bottle smashers, rapacious brigands and sabre-toothed tigers.

The trouble is that we still produce the same reactions to worrying stimuli which we can neither flee nor physically fight. You could of course flee from the college examinations you have to sit in a month's time; you could challenge your boss to a bout of fisticuffs when he did not give you a rise; and you could throw your typewriter out of the window when it prints 'sausage' instead of 'assuage' ten times in a row. Unfortunately such tactics do not aid survival in a world of smooth-mannered technocracy. What was a sensible habit in the era of sabre-toothed tigers now becomes useless. And if we continually react to unwelcome stimuli by pushing up our blood pressure we develop a useless habit which is distinctly unhealthy.

When I described the rigours of my journey to Croydon to Dr Patel, she gently suggested that if I did not succumb to hypertension I would probably get myself killed in a road accident. Driving is a typical stressful activity. The fight or flight mechanism is constantly being triggered, but instead of following the promptings of the sympathetic nervous system you sit in your jam jar and stew. One of the first things Dr Patel teaches her patients is to welcome red traffic lights as an opportunity to relax and practice their breathing exercises – *not* to act like it was a matador's cape and practice your Spanish bull-pawing-the-dust routine on the accelerator pedal.

Because conventional medicine has not endorsed the stress theory, it has sought to treat hypertension by straightforward allopathic methods. There are currently more than 50 drugs on the market being prescribed for hypertension. Most act by blocking nerves which stimulate the heart or make blood vessels contract. When correctly prescribed they do their job well, but they have a number of side-effects which include diarrhoea, impotence, blurred vision, stuffy nose and feeling faint when you get up from your chair or bed. The best way to judge a theory is by its results, rather than its assumptions. If hypertension is caused by stress, you would expect that by reducing stress you could bring down the blood pressure.

Although stress may seem a vague and subjective state of affairs, it can be broken down into several elements, some of which can be measured electronically. The electroencephalograph (EEG) is a device which measures electrical activity in the brain. Electrodes are placed on the subject's scalp (in animal experiments and in some brain operations they are placed inside the brain itself) and the electrical activity is monitored by a moving needle or a pen which moves up and down and records the electrical waves on a rolling sheet of graph paper.

Unless the electrodes are actually implanted in the brain it is really rather difficult to judge just where all this activity is being generated. However, in the 1930s Berger discovered that certain frequencies were associated with various states of consciousness. He placed an electrode on the back of his subject's head and picked up an electrical rhythm of about ten cycles a second. When Berger attached that electrode, his volunteer was not concentrating on anything in particular, just daydreaming. When the volunteer opened his eyes and paid attention to what was going on around him Berger noticed that the brainwave frequency shot up. That first rhythm, which occurred when the mind was 'out of gear', fluctuated between 7 and 13 cycles a second. Berger named it 'alpha' – because it was the first rhythm he had discovered – and labelled the second rhythm, which was associated with concentration and activity, 'beta'. Beta rhythms fluctuate from 14 to 25 cycles, depending on how aroused the brain is.

As well as alpha and beta rhythms, there are theta, which range from about four to seven cycles, and delta, which range from one to four. Delta rhythms occur in deep sleep or in parts of the brain which have been damaged. Theta rhythms occur in trance or when you are just on the point of falling asleep. They are also associated with deep meditation and the 'creative' state of mind of an artist or healer. When the mind is aroused and the fight or flight mechanism triggered, brain-wave rhythms peak into the high beta levels.

Other methods of measuring arousal are the electromyograph and the galvanic skin potential recorder. The electromyograph, EMG for short, is a device which records the discharges of nerves in muscle and the resulting muscle contractions. In other words, it measures tenseness. The galvanic skin potential recorder measures the conductivity of the skin. When the sympathetic nervous system is stimulated, glands in the skin release small amounts of sweat, which are imperceptible to the eye and may not even be felt but are enough to markedly increase conductivity of the surface of the skin.

A high skin resistance is therefore an indicator of relaxation, and during the day that resistance will fluctuate considerably. A striking example of this has been shown by the psychologist and electronics engineer Maxwell Cade who tested the skin resistance of patients at the Chelsea Hospital for Women. When they were under anaesthetic, lying on the trolley waiting to be wheeled into the operating theatre and about as relaxed as they could ever be, their skin resistance was 10 million ohms per square centimetre. Earlier, however, when they were conscious, about to be given their injections, and could hear the clink of the instruments in the sterilizer, fearful anticipation brought their skin resistance down to just 1000 ohms.

The EMG and skin resistance device work through electrodes which are attached to the skin. Muscle contraction or changes in resistance are shown either by a needle on a dial or by a loudspeaker which registers tension by emitting a variable high-pitched tone.

The EEG, the EMG and the skin resistance devices are the basic tools of biofeedback. Literally, biofeedback means feedback from life. It is a mechanical means of telling you what is going on inside your body.

So, if we have this information, what can we do with it? How is it going to help bring down the blood pressure?

The answer is that by becoming aware of what the body is doing, we can learn to control it. For centuries it has been known that Indian yogis and swamis can do all kinds of amazing things with their bodies. It was only when Western scientists had invented EEGs, electrocardiograms and all their other measuring apparatus that they realized that yogis who claimed to be able to stop their heartbeat or have themselves sealed up in airtight tanks for hours on end were not hoaxing.

In 1971 Dr Elmer Green, director of the Psychophysiology Laboratory of the Menniger Foundation in Topeka, Kansas, performed a number of tests on an Indian called Swami Rama. As well as demonstrating telepathetic and psychokinetic skills (he was able, amongst other things, to make a cyst appear on his thigh, disappear and reappear on other spots) Swami Rama, while connected to an ECG, showed that he could alter his heartbeat at will from 66 beats a minute, up to 94 and back to 52. Dr Green had seen similar feats performed before, but he had initially been interested to test the Swami because a colleague had told him that he could make his pulse disappear altogether.

Swami Rama told Green that he usually needed to fast for three days before attempting this stunt. But as time was pressing, and as the Swami's own teacher had been able to stop his heartbeat at will, he agreed to try it without taking the normal preparations. He offered to stop his heart for three or four minutes, but Green cautiously suggested that ten seconds would be quite enough for his purposes.

At the beginning of the test the Swami's heart rate was 70 beats a minute. The ECG recording of the test showed that it suddenly rose to 300 beats for a period of 17 seconds.

Dr Green was perplexed. The Swami claimed to have stopped his heart, while the ECG appeared to have registered quite the opposite, an unbelievably fast rate. He took the ECG printout to a cardiologist for a second opinion and was told that a rate of 300 per minute was a condition known as 'atrial flutter'. It happened when the heart was not pumping blood and its valves were not working. The 'flutter' was a reflex movement in the heart's empty chambers; blood pressure dropped and the person invariably fainted. 'What happened to your patient?' he asked.

Green had to tell him that the Swami had taken off his electrodes and gone off to give a lecture.

During other tests performed during the same session the Swami had shown that he was able simultaneously to raise the temperature of a spot just below the little finger and make it fall on a spot just below the thumb of the same hand. He managed to effect a difference of eleven degrees fahrenheit between the two areas.

To develop Swami Rama's skills you would need to study yoga for at least fifteen years under a teacher who had achieved similar control himself. However, physiological measurements made of people who are only reasonably proficient at practising yoga have shown that while they are relaxed they decrease their oxygen consumption, reduce carbon dioxide excretion when breathing out, and bring down their heart rate, respiratory rate, blood pressure, blood cortisone levels, blood lactate levels and reduce muscle tension. Skin resistance increases, the flow of blood (though not the pressure) goes up and the skin temperature of their extremities rises. All these phenomena are the exact opposite of what happens when you are under stress. The beta rhythms which are a sign of arousal in the brain give way to the slower alpha rhythms.

For a general practitioner like Chandra Patel, hypertension is a routine, but worrying, problem. It is dangerous but often has no symptoms, and the drugs used to control it are effective but have unpleasant side-effects too. Deciding which drug is right for which patient can take weeks of trial and error.

The first serious attempt to apply yoga techniques to clinical medicine and give a scientific assessment of the results was made by Professor K. K. Datey of Bombay University. In 1969 he and his colleagues found that the yogic technique *Shavasan* could reduce high blood pressure. In Britain yoga is a thing people do in evening classes, not the doctor's surgery. This is a pity, because with its concentration on posture and good breathing it could almost certainly prevent many of the minor respiratory problems and backache which come the way of the GP. But most people think yoga has got something to do with sticking your left foot up behind your right ear. They go to the doctor for medicine, not to be told to become contortionists.

We are all fascinated by machines, though, especially if we can operate them ourselves. This fascination does prompt us to hurl ourselves to heaven in motor cars and motor bikes, but in other aspects it is demonstrably healthy. Epileptic children attached to EEG machines have been so fascinated by the wavy lines their brain makes the instrument print that they have been taught to control the 'spiky' patterns of activity which are symptomatic of a seizure. Just how they manage to alter their brainwaves is a mystery, but the fact remains that once they have been shown a picture of their disease in the form of an EEG graph, they can learn to modulate it. These abilities are probably not so much the product of willpower as of intuition.

Maxwell Cade has found that most of his experimental volunteers can make the skin temperature of their fingers rise by a few degrees with a little coaching. When they start the exercise, they are just told 'Make your fingers get hotter'. They generally fail miserably because they concentrate too hard, push adrenalin into their system and elicit the *drop* in temperature which normally accompanies the fight and flight response. Only when they are told to stop willing it to happen, to relax and *imagine* it happening, does the temperature begin to rise.

Professor Datey's success with yoga and a few hopeful laboratory studies of biofeedback reported from the USA made Chandra Patel think it might be a good idea to combine the two techniques. In her Croydon practice she had plenty of hypertensive patients who could benefit. None of them admittedly were adepts of yoga, but to make things simple she devised a relaxation programme which involved nothing outlandish like sticking their feet behind their ears.

For biofeedback she decided to use an inexpensive skin resistance recorder called, aptly enough, The Relaxometer. This consists of a little black box, battery operated, with a small loudspeaker inside it. The patient is wired to the machine with electrodes which are fixed to two fingers with a piece of tape. The tiniest amount of sweat released by the glands in the fingers causes an immediate increase in the conductivity of the skin. When this happens the loudspeaker emits a high bleeping tone which becomes more and more intense as sweat is released and resistance falls.

The device is similar in principle to a lie detector, which also picks up sweat gland activity. The idea is that if the person being interviewed is telling the truth he will be calm. When he lies, he tenses up, his sympathetic nervous system activates the sweat glands, and the resulting change in resistance is noticed by the interrogator.

For her trial Dr Patel took 20 patients from her practice, all but one of whom were already being prescribed drugs for their hypertension. The remaining patient had high blood pressure, but she was taking other medications for depression and thyroid problems. Whenever attempts had been made in the past to reduce the patients' drug dose, the only result had been a rise in their blood pressure. A few of them had only had their high blood pressure diagnosed within the last eighteen months, while others had been hypertensive for ten years or more.

Dr Patel got her patients to come to the surgery three times a week for three months. Each of them got half an hour of individual attention. The session began with a blood pressure reading. The patient would then lie on the examination couch with legs slightly apart, arms by the side, palms upwards and fingers slightly flexed. They would be attached to the relaxometer.

They would then be told to pay attention to their breathing, making sure it was smooth and regular. They would then mentally go over the muscles of various parts of the body, face neck, abdomen, chest, to check that nothing was tense. So that the relaxation did not send them to sleep they would be told to repeat a phrase like 'My arms are feeling heavy and relaxed', or to concentrate on the rhythm of their breathing. Concentrating mentally while totally relaxing the body was intended to keep them alert, to make them feel in control of themselves.

Meanwhile, if they really were relaxing the tone of the relaxometer would fade gradually away, to an occasional beep, and finally to nothing at all. At the end of the session their blood pressure would be recorded again.

So that they did not leave the surgery only to plunge themselves straight back into the stressful habits of life, they were given a cassette tape with a recording of simple relaxation exercises to practice at home. Those who did a lot of driving were urged to practice their breathing exercises at red traffic lights. Anyone who wore a watch was given a little red sticker to stick on the face.

'Whenever you see the red dot, it's time to relax,' Dr Patel would tell them.

When the trial period of three months was up, all but four of the patients had reduced their blood pressure to a greater or lesser degree. Five patients had also been able to give up their anti-hypertensive drugs altogether, and seven others had reduced their drug intake by between 33 and 60 per cent. The lady with thyroid problems had given up her anti-depression drugs and reported that her migraine attacks had abated considerably.

All things considered it seemed to be a success. But success in medicine is not success unless it lasts. How long were the good effects going to last? And how much of the benefit could be attributed to the kind attention they had been receiving from the doctor. In general practice the average consultation time is six minutes. They had been getting half an hour three times a week.

Ten years earlier American doctors in Tennessee had found that they had been able to reduce the blood pressure of two groups of patients for three months equally by giving one group a popular antihypertensive drug and by giving the other group an inert placebo. Obviously many patients could bring down their blood pressure without drugs. The Americans had also found that the patients with the highest blood pressures tended to achieve the greatest reductions.

Dr Patel followed up her 20 patients for another nine months. They just came in to see her once a month instead of three times a week but were encouraged to keep practising the relaxation.

She then selected another 20 patients with hypertension, matching them for age and sex with the first 20. As there was no shortage of matchable patients with high blood pressure, and as she did not want to be accused of deliberately choosing patients who would suit her purposes best, she chose for the second group patients of the same age and sex whose names began with the same or the nearest alphabetical letter to the members of group one. The second group were not instructed in relaxation. They had their blood pressure taken at the beginning and end of the consultation, and for the rest of the time they just lay on the couch doing nothing in particular.

The aim of the exercise was to see whether the second group would have reduced their blood pressure as much as the first group had. They didn't. Indeed taken as a whole they did not show any significant change at all. But after twelve months the first group had managed to keep their blood pressure down to the same level they had achieved after the first three months of training.

The results of those two trials were published in *The Lancet* in November 1973 and January 1975 respectively. For good measure, and to make sure that favourable results were not just a quirk, Dr Patel was encouraged to do another trial with a completely different set of patients. Thirty-four people were chosen and randomly allocated to a 'treatment group' which got the whole works and a 'control group' who were given the placebo therapy, consisting of being told to relax and having their blood pressures taken regularly.

The results were as before. The treatment group reduced their collective blood pressure. Some members of the control group did too, but others did not, and yet others had their blood pressure go up.

At the end of six weeks the two groups swapped roles. The controls who had previously just been told to relax were now given biofeedback and taught to relax, while the former treatment group were left to their own devices. Six weeks later the average blood pressure of both groups was almost exactly the same. Those who had just learnt biofeedback and relaxation had brought down their blood pressure, and those who had finished their course six weeks earlier had maintained their reduction. The technique appeared to work.

High blood pressure is not the only result of stress. Many substances, notably sugar and fats, get pumped into the bloodstream when the fight or flight trigger goes off. In their book *Type A Behaviour and Your Heart* the American doctors Friedman and Roseman report a study which was made of accountants during the months of January to June in one year. The busiest time of the year for accountants is April when the tax deadline draws near.

What the doctors found was that as April came closer the level of cholesterol in the accountants' blood rose ever steeper. Come May and June when the worst of the year's work was done, they had little to worry about except how to spend their money for the next six months. Their cholesterol levels dropped. The fluctuation could not be explained by changes in their diet or other habits – only, apparently, by the fact that they had been under stress.

Cholesterol is a white, fat-like substance which occurs in most animal tissues. When it reaches high levels in the blood it may contribute to the development of heart disease. The amount of cholesterol in the blood is usually, though not always, found to be high in people suffering from heart disease, angina and stroke; and it is argued that an excess of cholesterol contributes to the furring up of arteries which leads to these complaints. Opponents of this theory declare that the evidence is only circumstantial. You almost always find vultures circling around a dead elephant, but that does not mean that the vultures killed it.

Whatever the truth may be, there are now millions of people being advised by their doctors to avoid foods, like eggs, which contain lots of cholesterol. Drugs have also been used to reduce cholesterol levels, but they seem to have had little effect in reducing heart disease. High blood pressure, smoking, diabetes, overweight and lack of physical exercise have all been associated with heart disease too. Once again there is no proof that they cause the disease, but the statistics show that people who have one or more of those 'risk factors' are – statistically, at least – more likely to get heart attacks.

Every three minutes someone in Britain dies of heart disease. That chilling statistic has prompted the Royal College of Physicians to suggest that doctors should put aside their theoretical arguments about what causes the disease and attack it from every possible angle. The most powerful weapon in this attack cannot be drugs. Heart disease is not an infection you pick up on the bus; it is the result of bad habits which only the patient can change.

A link between stress and heart disease has been noticed by generations of doctors. At the beginning of this century Sir William Osler described his angina patients (angina is a severe pain in the chest symptomatic of a failure in the coronary arteries to supply blood to the heart muscles) as robust, vigorous, keen and ambitious men, 'the indicators of whose engines are always set at full speed ahead'. In 1945 Kemple typified the heart patient as an aggressive, ambitious individual with intense physical and emotional drive, who found it hard to delegate responsibilities to others. In 1958 S. G. Wolf expanded this description by noting that such patients reacted vigorously to challenge but derived little satisfaction from their accomplishments. And nearly 200 years ago John Hunter, the founder of British surgery, wrote about 'Affections of the Heart upon every occasion which agitated the mind'. Hunter is remembered for his prophetic statement that his life was in the hands of 'any scoundrel who can put me in a passion'. Poor Hunter met his end at what must have been a very stressful meeting of the St George's Hospital board. According to his biographer, Hunter arrived at the hospital apparently in good health, but 'meeting with some things which irritated his mind, and not being perfectly master of the circumstances, he withheld his sentiments, in which state of restraint he went into the next room and turning round to Dr Robertson, one of the physicians of the Hospital, he gave a deep groan and dropped down dead.'

Back in twentieth-century Croydon Dr Patel teamed up with Dr Malcolm Carruthers, a pathologist at St Mary's Hospital, to see whether her therapy could be applied to the prevention of heart disease. After her initial success with blood pressure she carried out another small trial with another group of her patients to see whether cholesterol levels responded to bio-feedback and relaxation as well as hypertension did. In 1976 she was able to report in the *Journal* of the Royal College of General Practitioners that thirteen out of fourteen patients had been able to reduce their cholesterol levels by ten per cent as well as their hypertension.

Bearing in mind that the Royal College of Physicians was urging a 'multifactorial approach' to heart disease, she and Dr Carruthers went on to test whether the technique could affect any of the other risk factors.

A notice was duly stuck up in the waiting room of the surgery premises she shared with three other GPs. Volunteers aged between 25 and 60 were invited to take part in a 'heart disease research programme'.

The 76 volunteers were a mixed bunch. Thirty-six of them did not have high blood pressure. Eighteen of them were smokers who had had the habit for more than five years or who were already trying to wean themselves from nicotine by taking part in the practice's 'anti-smoking clinic'. Of the remaining 22, all had hypertension, twelve were on drugs and ten were not.

So that they would have a human yardstick against which they could assess the results of treatment, the doctors divided the lucky patients who did not have high blood pressure into two groups, one of which did not get any coaching in relaxation and biofeedback.

Dr Patel had been given paid study leave to do this trial, but it would not have been possible to give nearly 60 individuals the same kind of attention her patients had received in earlier trials. Training had to be carried out in groups of four, and each group came along to a single half hour session every week for six weeks. The patients were loaned cassette recorders with a tape of relaxation exercises to do at home once or, preferably, twice a day.

The smokers responded dramatically. After one week they had cut their cigarette consumption by 45 per cent. After six weeks it was down on average 80 per cent. When the six week course was over some of them slipped back into their old habits; nevertheless, when they were all followed up at the end of six months, the average number of cigarettes they smoked was just ten a day, compared with over 26 when they had begun training.

All the groups except those who had received no coaching achieved a significant reduction in blood pressure. The smokers and hypertensive experienced a marked reduction in their cholesterol levels. The hypertensive group and the treated volunteers who did not have high blood pressure also showed a significant reduction in the amount of triglycerides and free fatty acids in their blood.

All this had been achieved without the patients having to diet, take more exercise or change their job. By 'thinking healthy' they were making themselves healthier.

There is now just one big question which remains to be answered. How much has Dr Patel's personal enthusiasm contributed to the success of the biofeedback training? Pioneers of many therapies, good and bad, have managed to get results which could not be matched by those who followed. A much larger trial is now being carried out in Oxford involving several doctors and scores of patients. If that succeeds – and we shall not know until 1980 – the much maligned concept of 'self-control' should be back in fashion.

6 Autogenics/Psychic Diagnosis—Pain Pain go Away

Slumped back in an armchair in a drab hospital office is a plump, stocky young man wearing a short-sleeved shirt and no shoes. He has electrodes attached to his head, wrists and feet. The room is small, crowded and hot. In the gaps left between the cupboards, bookshelves and the cumbersome pieces of electrical equipment, nine other people have pressed themselves into tight vantage points to view the proceedings. A broken Coca Cola bottle lies in pieces in the middle of the floor.

'Okay, doc, what's next on the list?' the young man asks. 'I guess it must be the matches.'

'Right. The matches,' replies the doctor, a lean man wearing a bright check shirt and string tie. 'Who has the matches?'

One of the photographers sitting behind the doctor reaches into an ill-assorted pile of metal objects beside him. A pair of pliers. Three packs of stainless steel needles. A hammer. A 1lb can of Libby's fruit cocktail. A spring-loaded animal trap. A penknife. And the matches, which he passes to the doctor.

The young man holds out his left hand. The doctor tears one of the cardboard matches from the book and tries to light it. The end bends, the flame gutters, and the doctor flicks it to the floor before it can burn him.

'Haven't we any decent matches?' he asks. Someone throws him a small box of stick matches. The young man is still sitting there with his hand stuck out.

The doctor strikes a match, lets the flame reach a good threequarters of an inch in height, and then runs the flame round the young man's palm. It leaves a brown mark two inches long and half an inch wide across the ball of the young man's thumb. The flame burns towards the end of the match-stick and begins to burn the doctor's finger.

'Yow!' He flicks the match to the floor. 'I felt that even if you did not. Shall we try that again?'

'Okay,' says the young man.

The electrical apparatus to which the young man is connected are an electroencephalograph (EEG), which records electrical activity in the brain, an electrocardiograph (ECG) to measure heart activity, a Galvanic Skin Potential recorder which picks up changes in the electrical conductivity of the skin, and a thermometer electrode which records the surface temperature of the skin. All the bodily functions which are being recorded are controlled by the autonomic nervous system, that part of the nervous system which we might compare with an automatic pilot. These bodily functions are generally believed to operate beyond our conscious control, by reflex rather than by a constant effort of will. In other words, involuntary, rather than voluntary.

When the doctor has repeated the match test, the young man offers to perform a few more demonstrations. He takes a lighted cigarette, opens his mouth wide, and stubs it hard on his tongue. He takes a steel needle which he pushes through an inch of muscle in his upper arm. When the tip of the needle pops through on the other side he pulls it through with the pliers and sticks it back through again the other way. The hapless observers exchange glances, revealing disgust, horror, fascination.

The young man gets up, rolls up his trouser legs, and delights us all by walking on the broken glass. For good measure he jumps up and down on it a few times. He then asks to be given the penknife, a none too clean object of Swiss manufacture, with a blunt blade. Holding the knife in his right hand, he scrapes the blade through the skin just below the nail of his left middle finger. Having removed a strip of skin about a quarter of an inch deep and as wide as the finger, he goes on to perform the same insalubrious operation on another finger. Although the doctor reports that he has cut through and removed the epidermis and dermis, the fingers hardly bleed.

The animal trap which has been provided for the experiment has smooth rather than serrated metal jaws. It is the kind popular with poachers and trappers who hunt for furry mammals like fox and beaver, and is powerful enough to break an animal's leg instantly. The trap is set. The young man plunges his hand into it, and the jaws clamp across his palm and the back of his hand just below the finger joints.

As one of the observers releases him from the contraption, the young man admits: 'I did feel that, but in a strange kind of a way. It wasn't pain, just a kind of pressing.' There are no bruises or cuts on the hand.

He then asks for another object from the pile, a small steel rod three inches long and about one-twentieth of an inch in diameter. He lifts back his head, holds the rod directly in front of one eye, and quickly pushes it up to the hilt under his eyeball into the socket. He blinks a few times. As he withdraws the rod a big tear rolls down his cheek.

The doctor points out that by sticking the rod where he did there was not too much chance of doing serious damage as there is a layer of fatty tissues between the socket and the eyeball. 'Nevertheless, I don't think it is the kind of thing I would try on myself.'

For his *pièce de résistance*, the young man called for the 1lb tin of fruit cocktail (you must have wondered what that was for). Standing up, he placed two fingers of his left hand on the wooden arm of his chair, at just below waist height. Taking the can of fruit cocktail in his right, he raised his arm above his head and then smashed the heavy can down on his fingers. Smash. Smash. Smash. Three times.

The can was buckled by a dent two inches deep. The fingers were unharmed, not even bruised, let alone broken. In fact the only wounds the young man had sustained from the whole demonstration were the scorch on his hand from the burning match – which he had not felt – a few small punctures in his feet from splinters of glass, and the self-inflicted abrasions below his fingernails. The only thing he had complained of when stubbing cigarettes out on his tongue was the unpleasant taste of the burnt tobacco. The cuts below his fingernails had healed within three hours. He had made that demonstration at quarter to three in the afternoon. When the doctor examined his fingers again at a quarter to six, skin had reformed and there was only a slight vascularity – redness – to show that the damage had ever been done. Normally such cuts would take at least three days to heal properly.

The young man who so happily subjected himself to these outrages on his body – the demonstration took place at St Francis's Hospital, La Crosse, Wisconsin, on 6 January 1978 – is William Neal, a 29-year-old American and self-taught psychic, who has begun to make a name for himself demonstrating his pain-resistant faculty and other psi abilities to large audiences in the United States.

The doctor is Norman Shealy, a neurosurgeon by training, and one of the United States's leading experts on the treatment of intractable pain. It was he who discovered or, more exactly, rediscovered that electrical stimulation of nerves could relieve pain in a number of highly unpleasant diseases which had until the early 1970s been almost completely untreatable. In 1967 he designed a device called the dorsal column stimulator, which consisted of an electrode implanted into the spine, attached to a tiny portable control box which could be operated by the patient. These devices are now used throughout the world and have brought considerable relief to people suffering from severe back pain, phantom limb pain resulting from amputation, and multiple sclerosis. He also pioneered the much simpler technique of transcutaneous electrical stimulation, by which electrodes are placed on the skin and a very low voltage current passed through them. This is now a standard treatment for backache and the pain caused by shingles.

But more recently Dr Shealy has developed a completely new approach to treating his patients, almost all of whom suffer from chronic intractable pain which has resisted the treatment of the whole gamut of medical specialists. Instead of treating his patients by giving them drugs or operations, he teaches them to get rid of their pain by controlling their autonomic nervous system, that part of the nervous system which, as I mentioned earlier, is widely believed to be beyond our conscious control. He also avails himself of the services of clairvoyants and healers, people with whom conventional medics would not dare or care to be associated. Leaving aside for a moment the psychic aspects of Dr Shealy's work, the central elements of the lessons he offers his patients are biofeedback and autogenics. He combines the two methods into a pain control therapy which he calls biogenics.

I had better make it clear that William Neal's demonstration is not typical of what Shealy claims biogenics can do for pain relief. It has more in common with a circus act than a medical therapy, and Dr Shealy warns that individuals who subject their autonomic nervous systems to the kind of strains that Neal is imposing will probably shorten their lives rather than enhance them. But the fact that Neal can switch himself off from sudden acute pain does dramatically illustrate Shealy's ideas about the possibilities of pain control open to the most hopeless sufferers.

Very rarely, children are born who do not feel pain. Something is missing somewhere in their nervous system. One might think that it is a shame more of us do not have this deficit and cannot be spared the aggravation of a thousand complaints from toothache to chronic arthritis. But of course pain does have an important function as a warning system. The children who do not feel pain invariably end up doing themselves dreadful damage. One little girl was found by her mother burning her knees on a stove, quite unaware that she was hurting herself. Others have been oblivious to broken bones and swollen joints and have thus inadvertently destroyed their limbs. Acute pain is unpleasant but very necessary. Unnecessary pain is the kind of chronic pain which accompanies backache or cancer. It just goes on and on relentlessly, long after its initial important warning message has been understood by the sufferer. And it is chronic pain which Dr Shealy seeks to conquer.

The tests on William Neal revealed that he was manipulating

his autonomic system in a bizarre fashion. The electroen-
cephalogram showed that just before he attempted one of his
stunts he induced, very briefly, alpha rhythms in his brain.
Normally alpha rhythms are brought on by meditation,
hypnosis or prolonged relaxation, but Neal could apparently
switch them on and off very quickly. The fact that he was not
in an alpha state the whole time indicated that he was not in a
trance. In the alpha state the brain does not usually perceive
pain. However, the kind of concentration Neal was bringing
to his performance would usually elicit nothing but higher
frequency beta waves in the brain.

The Galvanic Skin Potential recorder showed that the conductivity of his skin decreased just before he did a stunt. High
conductivity is an indicator of tension. The GSP readings,
together with the electrocardiogram which showed that his
pulse was very high during the whole performance, suggested
that he was very keyed up. His pulse remained more or less
constant at about 120 a minute, almost twice the normal
healthy pace. It was still racing three hours later.

The skin temperature gauge showed that he was switching
quickly from relaxation to concentration. A high skin temperature tends to indicate relaxation: we have seen how migraine
sufferers are taught consciously to raise their skin temperature
to reduce tension and ward off headache attacks. During the
tests Neal's skin temperature ranged widely between 84 and
94 degrees fahrenheit. Just before he embarked on one of his
stunts the temperature would rise but would tend to fall
quite sharply afterwards.

Neal is not one of those people with a congenital inability
to feel pain. If you pinched him when he was not expecting it,
he would squeal like anyone else. As a boy, he told me, he was
'super-sensitive' to pain and would complain about every little
knock. He says that he simply taught himself to be able to turn
pain off when he wanted to. When he does his stunts, for
instance, he does not think of his body at all – 'I only think of
the pliers or the needle. It is as if my arm did not exist.'

Dr Shealy points out that there are positive and negative
sides to William Neal's extraordinary ability. It is not very

healthy to have your pulse racing away at 120 a minute for hours on end. However, by training himself not to feel pain, Neal has also developed another remarkable skill, that of being able to heal himself very rapidly. He shares this ability with other psychics, notably Jack Schwartz, who was studied by Dr Elmer Green and who was able to staunch the flow of blood from a self-inflicted wound just by saying 'Now it stops'. Control of the autonomic nervous system would seem to offer medicine some far-reaching possibilities.

Although Norman Shealy had won himself a world-wide reputation among fellow neurosurgeons for his inventions of the dorsal column stimulator and transcutaneous nerve stimulator, he was not content that these methods were really what patients with chronic pain needed. His discontent grew when he saw electrical stimulators being pushed commercially as a panacea for pain.

He was also concerned that neurosurgery was generally causing as many, or even more, problems than it solved.

One of the most popular operations for back pain – with surgeons, if not with patients – is laminectomy. The operation consists of removing a layer of bone in the spinal column to relieve pressure on the spinal cord, as it is thought that the pressure of bone on nerve is the cause of pain. This operation only really succeeds for about one patient in five, and just as many patients subsequently find that their pain actually gets worse.

Nor was Shealy convinced that his colleagues working in this field of chronic pain relief were doing their patients much good either. He describes their methods as 'block, cut, drug and shrink'. First the patient is given a nerve 'block' by the injection of local anaesthetic into the spine. If this succeeds in bringing temporary relief, the nerves which appear to be the origin of the pain may be cut surgically. Alternatively, or additionally, the patient may be given a drug régime, which can before long lead to dependence or addiction. As a last resort the patients are sent off to a psychiatrist to find out why they are so hung up.

'If these methods worked, I would never have gotten into

what I do now,' he declares. 'But the fact is that the patients get worse.'

In August 1971 he visited Dr Wilbert Fordyce, a clinical psychologist at the University of Washington in Seattle, who had been making a study of a technique called 'operant conditioning' on patients with intractable pain.

Briefly, Fordyce's technique consisted of ignoring the patient as long as he kept complaining of pain. First he would fully examine the patient to ensure that there was no physical disability which could prompt the amount of pain which he was complaining of. Fordyce would then withdraw the patient's drugs and propose a not particularly rigorous schedule of exercises. If the patient persisted in complaining of pain or lay down and refused to do the exercises, the staff were instructed to ignore him. Only when he stopped mentioning his pain and acted like a good boy did they encourage him to adopt a more friendly attitude.

Over a period of five years about 100 patients went through this two-month course which cost them 5000 dollars each. Sixty per cent of them, amazingly enough, actually got a lot better. They no longer felt their pain to anything like the extent they had previously, and had managed to get themselves off drugs. The effect did not always last; six months after discharge only 25 per cent of the women and 40 per cent of the men were still largely pain free and happy. Overall, however, a third of the patients had got better simply by being ignored, and had managed to stay better for more than six months, which showed that the benefits could not just be written off as a placebo response.

'If you could make a third of your patients better by doing what I regard as nothing, I guessed that you must be able to get even better results if you introduced a few safe therapies,' Shealy recalls. He therefore introduced a programme at St Francis's Hospital, La Crosse, which was based on operant conditioning, but with the addition of acupuncture, transcutaneous stimulation, massage, exercise, ice treatments and hydrotherapy. 'We added a little negative reinforcement too. If a patient kept going on about his pain, I would tell him to "cut the crap". And in general they did stop complaining and felt better for it.'

Biofeedback was brought into the La Crosse programme in 1973 after Shealy had heard Elmer Green talk about its effect on migraine at a medical conference in Phoenix, Arizona. 'I asked Elmer whether it would work for other kinds of pain. He said he did not know because no one had tried it. I asked him how I should set about it, and he told me that I would have to experiment.'

Without honestly knowing what he was letting himself or his patients in for, Shealy equipped his clinic with an EMG, EEG and skin temperature gauge. Hardly anyone seemed to be getting any benefit from it at all at first, except a few paraplegic patients – and even they experienced widely varying degrees of success. One 60-year-old man took to it almost immediately. After practising on the EEG for 20 minutes a day for just two days, he was able to produce alpha waves by just detaching himself mentally. He would practise for 15 minutes and manage to rid himself of pain for up to four hours.

'It's as if I was throwing a switch in my head,' he told a bemused but delighted Dr Shealy.

Another patient, a young man, was extremely enthusiastic about the therapy but had to practise for a month before he could free himself of pain for only an hour. Eventually, after ten months, he managed to keep his pain at bay permanently by practising three times a day.

The results from biofeedback were only vaguely promising so far. Shealy decided that if self-conditioning was going to work more effectively, his patients would have to be exposed to it more thoroughly. It seemed a good idea to back up biofeedback with a therapy which could be called its emotional counterpart – autogenics.

Autogenics was invented in the 1920s by a German, Johannes H. Schultz. Schultz had found that sick or distressed people could learn to control a number of supposedly autonomic or involuntary functions by thought alone. If a person was allowed to sit quietly and say to himself 'My hands are getting warmer', his hands did indeed get warmer. In the same way he could produce a calm, regular heartbeat, a cool forehead, a warm abdomen. The same effects could be achieved under hypnosis, which Schultz had previously practised. The trouble with hypnosis, though, was that it was erratic. Some patients could be hypnotized, others could not. One reason for this appeared to be that some individuals were more resistant than others and would not let themselves fall into the hypnotic trance. With autogenics the individual was in complete control and did not have to feel that he was falling under the spell of a hypnotist. Autogenics is, in other words, biofeedback without the gadgetry. If you have not tried it, it may seem unbelievable that you can raise the temperature of your hand just by thinking. But you can. Even I can. Norman Shealy's twelve-year-old son managed to raise the skin temperature of his hand by 10°F at the first attempt.

Before Schultz had coined the term autogenics, a French pharmacist, Emil Coué, had pioneered a basically similar self-help therapy in 1910. He simply suggested that people should say to themselves the sentence 'Every day, in every way, I am getting better and better.'

A major problem for people with chronic pain is that they cannot relax. Shealy has found that a simple autogenic technique to induce relaxation is to imagine that your body, your whole body, has expanded by one inch. You do not push it out, you just let it expand of its own accord. Then you expand it by three inches, six inches, a foot. All round.

'You can't do this when you are tense,' Shealy says. 'So when you reach this feeling of expansion you've relaxed fully.'

Frequently, the more sceptical of Shealy's patients object to autogenics with its implication that 'everything, including your pain, is in your head'. Many of them have already had exhaustive consultations with psychiatrists and resent the implication that their pain is imaginary, or even worse, that they are just plain nuts. They want to be treated for a physical complaint, not to be told that they should treat themselves.

The answer he gives is that a whole multitude of diseases do have an emotional origin. The body can react to stress by pumping acid into the stomach. This is a normal physiological action, but when it happens too often the acid ends up burning a hole in the lining of the stomach and you get an ulcer. Worry and anticipation of an important event in the near future can make you constipated or give you diarrhoea. Asthma and high blood pressure can also often be explained as psychosomatic complaints. Psychosomatic does not mean 'all in the mind'; it means that the disease is the result of an interaction between mind and body. Asthma is very often brought on by an emotional disturbance, though no one who had witnessed a young asthmatic child fighting for breath would suggest that he was shamming his distress.

A great deal of chronic pain is also psychosomatic. There may well be a physical cause for some of the pain experienced by the sufferer, but anxiety and stress can magnify that pain to such an extent that it becomes the only thing the patient can think of. Pain understandably makes people anxious; anxiety in turn can reduce their tolerance of pain – and a vicious circle is established.

Stress could be described as a prolonged minor emotional disturbance, anger, fear or guilt which leads to chemical imbalance in the body. Dietary deficiencies or unhealthy habits like smoking, drinking alcohol and excessive consumption of coffee can upset the body's chemical balance too. By overcoming the emotional disturbances and correcting the deficiencies and bad habits, the patient can regain control of his body.

To anyone who still finds it hard to believe that he can control autonomic bodily functions, Dr Shealy points out that most people have managed to control two autonomic functions – urination and defecation – by the time they are three years old.

A basic autogenic exercise for pain relief could run so:

'Now relax, close your eyes, take a deep breath and repeat mentally to yourself each sentence after I say it.

'My arms and legs are heavy and warm. (6 times.)

'My heartbeat is calm and regular. (6 times.)

'My body breathes itself. (6 times.)

'My abdomen is warm. (6 times.)

'My forehead is cool. (6 times.)

'My mind is quiet and still. (3 times.)

'My mind is quiet and happy. (3 times.)

'I am at peace.

'I feel my feet expanding lightly and pleasantly by one inch. (2 times.)

'My feet are now expanding lightly and pleasantly by 12 inches. (2 times.)

'The pleasant 12 inch expansion is spreading throughout all the parts of my legs. (2 times.)

'My abdomen, buttocks and back are expanding 12 inches lightly and pleasantly. (2 times.)

'My chest is expanding 12 inches lightly and pleasantly. (2 times.)

'My arms are expanding 12 inches lightly and pleasantly. (2 times.)

'My neck and head are joining in the 12 inches of expansion. (2 times.)

'My entire body is relaxed, expanded and comfortable. (6 times.)

'My mind is quiet and still. (2 times.)

'I withdraw my mind from my physical surroundings. (2 times.)

'I am free of pain and all other sensations. (2 times.)

'My body is safe and comfortable. (6 times.)

'My mind is quiet and happy. (2 times.)

'I am that I am. (pause 2 minutes.)

'Each time I practise this exercise my body becomes more and more comfortable. And I carry this comfort with me to my normal awareness. As I prepare to return to my normal awareness I will bring with me the ideal comfort which I have created in my focused concentration. As I open my eyes, I take a deep comfortable breath and a big comfortable stretch.'

This exercise is quoted from Dr Shealy's book *The Pain Game*, Celestial Arts, Millbrae, California, 1976.

In 1975 the zealous administrator of St Francis's Hospital decided to triple the rent he charged to Shealy for his clinic. Shealy duly moved out of the hospital and built an extension to his farmhouse home which is set in a green and pleasant valley several miles out of town. (In winter the valley is snowy white and down to 40° below zero. Shealy claims that this does not noticeably affect the patients' chances of getting better, however.)

For the first two days of their twelve-day course, all 24 patients undergo three hours of 'indoctrination and orientation', followed by private consultations with two physicians and standard psychological personality tests. Thereafter, they have daily consultations with two or more of the clinic's staff, which includes a psychologist, physiotherapist, counsellor and nurse as well as the two doctors, and for the rest of their twelve-hour day they practice biofeedback and autogenics as a group. This is backed up by advice on nutrition, transcutaneous electrical stimulation and acupuncture. Towards the end of the course a few patients who obviously have pain with a diagnosable organic origin may be offered surgery. Shealy stresses that it is only a very small number who need this. A study of case histories from the past three years has shown that 90 per cent of the patients achieve 50 per cent to total pain relief, the greatest success being reported by patients with rheumatoid arthritis or paraplegic pain. Six months later, however, only 72 per cent are still wholly or partially pain free.

'Those who lapse do so because we have not been able to give them lasting faith,' Shealy explains. 'But considering that nearly everyone who comes here has had pain for at least six years and has already spent upwards of 50,000 dollars on medical treatment I think our figures are not bad.'

Faith is an important word in the Shealy canon. On a television discussion programme a doctor pejoratively described him as 'a faith healer'.

'He did not mean it as a compliment. But I took it as one.'

Faith healing in its more common meaning of laying-on-hands is not something he encourages, though. Firstly, it is a technique which makes the patient think that they can be cured by an outside force rather than by themselves. 'And secondly, I do not believe it works. Not for very long anyway.'

He has seen a number of demonstrations which might convince ordinary folk that paranormal healing did work. Henry Rucker, the clairvoyant healer who works as a counsellor at the centre, once healed all two dozen patients on one course by telling them that their pain was gone. And all two dozen immediately reported their pain had gone.

The next morning, all two dozen reported that their pain was back again.

For some ailments psychic healing may be effective. On one occasion Henry Rucker 'just kind of waved his hand' at some warts which were marring the hands of Shealy's elder son. 'He said they would be gone in three weeks – and they were!'

For chronic pain patients sterner stuff is needed, Shealy believes. 'Whatever the healing force may be, it has got to be internalized by the patients. They have to do the work. Hand healing may relieve pain for eight hours or so, but that's all in my experience. Even so, eight hours is twice as good as aspirin!' Shealy's involvement with Henry Rucker has led to their exploration of psychic faculties even more intriguing than faith healing. In the early 1970s Shealy had begun to get interested in the supposed ability of some claivoyants to diagnose disease. The late Edgar Cayce, the United States's most famous clairvoyant, in whose memory a large research institute has been established in Virginia Beach, had been able to diagnose illnesses of people brought to him when he was in a trance, and had been amazingly proficient at suggesting effective treatments for them too.

The first scientific paper on psychic diagnosis was presented by the English physician John Elliotson in London in 1842. Elliotson was a brilliant doctor and close friend of James Wakely, the first editor of *The Lancet*. Wakely's patronage had increased his reputation and had helped him towards becoming the first Professor of Medicine at University College,

London. Among other achievements Elliotson had been a pioneer in the use of narcotic drugs and had introduced the stethoscope to Britain.

During the 1830s he became intrigued by mesmerism, that remarkable and notorious early form of hypnotism which had resulted in its inventor, the Austrian doctor Franz Mesmer, being hounded from Vienna and Paris at the end of the eighteenth century. Elliotson tried practising Mesmer's techniques himself and made a number of public demonstrations. In one of these demonstrations he showed that mesmerised people became clairvoyant and could diagnose illnesses in individuals brought before them.

His involvement with so controversial a subject upset his medical colleagues who told him to give it up or resign. He chose the latter course and went into private practice. During the next ten years he developed the use of mesmerism as an anaesthetic for patients undergoing surgical operations.

The example of Cayce and other clairvoyants whom Shealy had come across made him want to test the diagnostic skills of clairvoyants more scientifically than had been done so far. He was recommended to contact Henry Rucker, a black healer and clairvoyant who, like many people with similar talents, had taken holy orders so that he could do his work with a minimum of harrassment from the authorities. (Goaded by the American Medical Association on the one hand and Fundamentalist Christians on the other, the American authorities pursue unorthodox practitioners with a zeal quite unknown in Britain since the witch hunts of Cromwellian times.)

'At our first meeting Henry told me things about myself which amazed me. He gave me facts about my life which even my wife did not know. He also told me that he had been expecting my arrival in his life for some time. He had had a dream about me,' Shealy recalls.

This auspicious beginning prompted Shealy to invite Henry Rucker and a few of his colleague psychics up to Wisconsin to see how their clairvoyant skills might relate to the patients in the clinic at St Francis's. He had previously warned his patients that the psychics were going to arrive and told them that anyone who did not want to be seen by them would not be asked to.

'No one refused. In fact they were almost falling over each other in anticipation.'

The psychic party included an astrologer, a numerologist, a palmist, a graphologist; the rest were clairvoyants. They were each allowed to see the individual patients but were told nothing about them and were not allowed to speak to them. All the information they received was a handwriting sample from each patient for the graphologist, their birth dates for the astrologer and numerologist, and a palm print for the palmist. Working from this information alone the psychics proved to be 80 per cent accurate in their diagnosis. They showed themselves able to give accurate accounts of the cause of pain, the site of the pain and details about the accident or event which caused it in the first place. Some were clearly more talented than others. Henry Rucker was shown one patient in whom Shealy had recently implanted a dorsal column stimulator. He had been worried about the patient because his white blood cell count had risen to the alarming level of 50,000 after the operation. Shealy was afraid that he might have stirred up a latent leukemia. He had arranged for a haemotologist to do a blood test, but he had not yet seen the specialist's report.

Henry Rucker took one glance at the man and said: 'It's not leukemia; it's a liver problem which will soon clear up. The man will be able to go home in ten days.'

Hearing this remarkable off-the-cuff declaration, Shealy's medical colleague in the clinic fetched the haemotologist's report. It confirmed Henry Rucker's diagnosis – and the man was indeed discharged just over a week later.

If an experiment is to have any scientific value it has to be repeated. Shealy decided that the next test of psychic diagnosis would have to be rigorously controlled by himself and a statistician who would check the likelihood of the results being the product of sheer chance.

For the second series of experiments the psychics were not even allowed to set eyes on the patients. All the clairvoyants were given was a photograph on the back of which Shealy's assistant had written the patient's name and birth date; the graphologist received one sheet of the patient's handwriting; and the palmist got a palm print. As a further control Shealy recruited a professor of psychology who claimed no psychic powers. He was just given a photograph with the patient's name and birth date, and asked to write down the first impressions which came into his head. Seventy-eight patients were involved.

The psychics were asked to say where the patient was suffering pain, and for this they were given a chart of the human body divided into twelve areas on the front of the body and ten on the back. They also had to state the cause, and for this they were given a choice of fourteen alternatives which included cancer, amputation, scar, stroke, infection, arthritis and so on.

The results were startling. The professor of psychology proved that he had no psychic talent. He was only five per cent accurate on guessing the cause of the pain. Two of the clairvoyants were 75 per cent accurate, and the third managed 70 per cent. The numerologist achieved 60 per cent, the astrologer 35 per cent, the palmist and graphologist 25 per cent. While the efforts of the latter two were really no better than guesswork or chance, the accuracy of the clairvoyants was statistically highly significant.

When it came to locating the pain the professor of psychology did a little better. He scraped ten per cent. The numerologist, astrologer, palmist and graphologist ranged between 30 and 50 per cent accuracy, while the clairvoyants managed 60 to 65 per cent.

An averagely competent doctor who had been able to give those patients a conventional physical examination could have been expected to achieve 80 to 90 per cent success. He would of course have had a little more evidence to go on. While not even Shealy suggests that clairvoyants should replace doctors for diagnosis, he suggests that they have a useful part to play in getting to the root of the trouble in difficult cases. He has found that their psychological insight can help the doctor enormously. In one case he cites a woman who had been bed-ridden for eight years and had responded extremely well to the clinic's therapy. Unfortunately her husband found it hard to relate to her new found well-being. He had been so used to supporting an invalid that he was not prepared to face a change in domestic life style. He had started picking fights with his wife and was threatening divorce. Shealy was at a complete loss as to how he could sort out this bizarre problem.

Henry Rucker was at the clinic one day when they came for a follow-up consultation, and Shealy, on the spur of the moment, suggested that the husband and wife talk things over with the 'visiting minister'. They agreed to this and went into conclave with Rucker for an hour and a half. When they came out the husband came up to Shealy and said: 'Doc, don't ever lose this man. He is the best thing you have got.'

It turned out that Rucker had divined secrets about their domestic life which they had not revealed to themselves, let alone to Shealy and the world at large. He began by telling them that their eldest son had been taking marijuana – a problem which had been preying on their minds but which they had not discussed openly before. He then made the husband almost swoon away by bringing up the matter of his mistress. This lady was obviously the stumbling block as far as the husband's relationship with his wife was concerned, although until then he had kept the matter strictly to himself.

When psychic gifts are combined with medical training, the dividends may be even greater. After making his study of clairvoyants' diagnostic abilities, Shealy learnt that psychiatrists in California had been employing a young physician, Bob Leichtmann, to do clairvoyant diagnoses to help them with difficult cases. All Leichtmann asked for was the patient's name, age and address or just a photograph, from which he was able to construct an accurate personality profile and pinpoint psychiatric disorders of the patient without ever seeing or talking to him.

Shealy had tested Leichtmann's skills for himself and claims that he can make personality assessments at a distance which are 96 per cent accurate. He supplied Leichtmann with the names and current addresses of 25 of his own patients, and when he got Leichtmann's profiles – which often run up to two or three typewritten pages – he found that he had made minor misjudgements of two individuals. Even in those cases the bulk of the personality analysis he supplied was otherwise quite sound.

Leichtmann's gift is not confined to divining personality, Shealy reports.

'Once I had a patient whose problems I just could not sort out. I called Bob on the phone, and he told me "Try L3". [L3 is the third vertebra in the lumbar region of the spine.] I pressed the patient's back at L3, and he shouted out: "That's the spot, doc!" I denervated the joint and got rid of a pain which had plagued that patient for 18 years.'

'I don't know how it works, but psychic diagnosis has very practical applications.'

Like radionics and radiesthesia, psychic diagnosis is one of those phenomena which, to be believed, require a rather radical reappraisal of one's conventional ideas about how the world works. Though I have not tested Dr Leichtmann's skills myself, I have heard them praised by apparently sane and honest medical men. Dr Shealy's experiments with other psychic diagnosticians ought to be repeated by a few more scientific observers, preferably in the United Kingdom where unquestioning belief in extra-sensory perception is not as rife as in the USA.

Biogenics is a novel approach to disease. The longer term value of the biofeedback element has been well established over almost a decade of experiment, though it does seem that some practitioners are better at teaching it than others and indeed that some patients are more prepared to learn it than others. Autohypnotic techniques which are not dissimilar to autogenic training are being used with success by some British doctors who specialize in treating intractable pain.

Without casting aspersions on Dr Shealy's claimed success, it is only reasonable to point out that any American doctor in private practice has a vested interest in boosting his therapies. British doctors working on a salary for the National Health Service may complain about their poor pay but do not have a financial incentive to cure their patients. Shealy is also an energetic man with a strong personality and ready wit, whose manner must at least encourage his patients.

As I pointed out in the chapter on healing, the doctor's charisma and the patient's desire to get better can be powerful forces for good, as strong as any drug. In the next chapter we look at another therapy which was until recently dismissed as nothing more than a placebo. But the critics who have bothered to study it have now had to shift their ground.

7 Acupuncture—Pains and Needles

Just in case anyone thinks that acupuncture is a new and largely untested innovation in Western medicine, I should draw your attention to a paragraph written by Sir William Osler in the eighth edition of the textbook *Principles and Practice of Medicine*, dated 1912.

> For lumbago, acupuncture is in acute cases the most efficient treatment. Needles from three to four inches in length, ordinary bonnet needles, sterilized, will do. They are thrusted into the lumbar muscles at the seat of pain, and withdrawn after five to ten minutes. In many instances the relief is immediate, and I can confirm fully the statements of Ringer, who taught me this practice, as to its extraordinary and prompt efficacy in many instances.

When Sir William, who was one of the most famous physicians of his day, wrote that, acupuncture had already been used in Britain and the United States for several decades. It was originally brought to Europe from China by French Jesuit priests.

Why acupuncture should have then disappeared almost entirely from European and American medical practice is something of a mystery. It was possibly due to the introduction of aspirin, first manufactured by the German chemical company Bayer in 1899. Aspirin is a very effective pain killer and anti-inflammatory drug which until very recently was the first drug specialists turned to when treating rheumatic and arthritic complaints. And, perhaps most important of all, aspirin comes as a pill. Patients the world over prefer pills to any other form of therapy; they are both painless and effortless to swallow. A few doctors continued to practise acupuncture in continental Europe, especially in France, but it did not regain its footing in Britain until Dr Felix Mann published his books on acupuncture in the early 1960s.

One of the most bewildering things about acupuncture is that you can hardly find two acupuncturists to agree about how the therapy actually works. Even the Chinese, who have been practising acupuncture for over 2500 years, have turned against their ancient theories and have still failed to come up with an explanation to satisfy themselves, let alone the rest of the world. There is no doubt that acupuncture does work – therapies need to be good if they are to last 2500 years – but just *how* it works is wide open to debate.

To understand modern Western medicine you do not have to know much about the work of ancient Greek, Roman and medieval European medical men. Hippocrates' oath is about the only tenet which survives, and that has come in for some battering of late. To understand acupuncture, however, you have to know something about Chinese theory and philosophy. The practices of most non-medically qualified acupuncturists are based almost exclusively on ancient Chinese techniques and beliefs, and even some of the medically qualified acupuncturists, who discard the classical theory, began by learning the ancient methods.

The ancient Chinese believed that a life force, Chi (also spelt, Chhi, Ki, Qi) flowed through all things. The flux of Chi was influenced by the forces of Yin and Yang, two polar principles which correspond very roughly to our notion of negative and positive, or female and male. The concept of Yin and Yang is difficult to translate; certain foods, substances or even places are said to be Yin, while others are Yang.

For a body to be healthy Yin and Yang must be in equilibrium, and it was the acupuncturists' task to restore that balance for the sick. Indeed the old Chinese acupuncturists did not confine themselves to curative medicine but recommended it for preventing disease too. This was a very practical professional strategy which ensured that they kept their fees coming in on a much more regular basis. It only backfired when the king caught a cold or the city went down with an epidemic, and the acupuncturists had to make themselves scarce for a few weeks.

According to classical theory Chi flows around the body along channels known as meridians. There are twelve major meridians, all but one of which are named after organs of the body. The six Yin organs are the liver, heart, spleen, kidney, lung and pericardium, while the six Yang organs are stomach, gall bladder, bladder, large intestine, small intestine and *sanjiao*, which is translated as 'triple warmer' but which does not correspond to any organ known to Western science. As well as these twelve meridians, there are two other important ones, the 'conception vessel' which runs up the front of the body from perineum to chin, and the 'governing vessel', which runs down the spine. (Note that they did not regard the brain as an important organ.)

When an acupuncturist assessed his patient, he would sit him down with his arms placed over a silken cushion and feel the pulse of each meridian. The pulses are found by feeling particular sections of the radial artery as it passes through the wrist; the pulses of six meridians are found on the left wrist, and six on the right. In Western medicine a doctor feels the radial pulse to find out the rate, force and rhythm with which the heart is pumping blood round the body. The traditional acupuncturist, however, looked for up to 27 different qualities in his patients' pulses. Having decided which meridians were out of kilter, he would take his needles and insert them at chosen spots along those meridians. By so doing he would restore the balance of Yin and Yang and get the Chi circulating at the proper healthy rate.

Various stories explain the origins of acupuncture in China, the most popular of which is that hunters and soldiers injured by arrows spontaneously recovered from ailments which had previously afflicted them. This rather 'hit or miss' form of therapy obviously bore more than acceptable iatrogenic risks. It was subsequently discovered that the site of the puncture, rather than the wound itself, was responsible for the beneficial side-effects.

The earliest non-mythical records of acupuncture date

from the Stone Age in China; they are inscribed on tortoise-shell and explain how flint needles were used to cure diseases. Jade and bamboo later became popular, and as Chinese metallurgy progressed, iron, bronze, silver and gold needles found their way into the acupuncturist's armoury. Yin and Yang properties were ascribed to various metals: silver, for instance, was regarded as Yin and thus used for its sedative effect, while the Yang qualities of gold made it more suitable for toning the system up. Steel needles are most commonly used today, and sedation or tonification of the system is achieved by twirling the needles clockwise or anticlockwise, respectively. As an alternative to needles practitioners some-times use a technique called moxibustion, which consists of putting small cones of the dried herb artemesia on the acu-puncture point, lighting it and letting it burn down almost to the skin.

By now you are doubtless totally confused, and I fear that your confusion will not be relieved by the mass of contra-dictory theorizing I now have to present.

The traditional Chinese theory of acupuncture is hard to swallow. Even if you are prepared to accept the existence of Chi, Yin and Yang, where, you may well ask, are these chan-nels through which this wondrous substance flows? They cannot be seen by naked eye or through microscope. Do they exist?

In 1965 a North Korean medical professor, Kim Bong Han, caused a major stir in the East when he claimed that he had found physical evidence that meridians existed. He produced photographs taken through a microscope which appeared to indicate the existence of a hitherto undiscovered physiological system. His findings greatly impressed the rulers of North Korea who showered him with honours and printed a series of postage stamps to celebrate the man and his work. His findings also interested the Chinese medical profession who had been trying to do the same thing for some years under the encourage-ment of Chairman Mao, whose father had been a herbalist and who was very keen to establish a scientific basis for tradi-tional Chinese medicine. A Chinese delegation duly visited

North Korea and was shown a series of dissected cadavers covered with an intriguing network of dyed-stained channels which did indeed resemble the meridians they had themselves been seeking. So they went home and tried to repeat Kim Bong Han's experiments for themselves. They were unable to do so.

Nor, indeed, has anyone else been able to do so. Chinese and European researchers who have tried agree that the only way Kim's channels could have got where they were was by being put there by Kim. Not a lot has been heard of the man of late. Rumour has it that he disappeared in mysterious circumstances.

Slightly more convincing evidence about meridians has come from researchers in France and the United States using electrical devices to measure skin resistance. They have found the electrical resistance of the skin is markedly lower on traditional acupuncture points than on the surrounding skin. This difference, while less strong, can also be found if an electrode is traced along the course of the meridians. The American surgeon, Professor Robert Becker of New York, who has made his own study of bioelectrical activity in the body, suggests that meridians and acupuncture points somehow resemble cables and generator stations in the body's electrical field.

Some psychics, notably the English healer Rose Gladden, report that they can see meridians, in the same way as a Buddhist can see a creature's aura or a Christian can see a saint's halo.

The ancient Chinese who charted meridians did not have Kim Bong Han's microscope and dyes, Becker's electrodes or Rose Gladden's psychic vision. (Some were perhaps psychic, but they could only have been a few among thousands.)

Nevertheless, there were some phenomena which they could describe which might have suggested the existence of channels. Acupuncture patients sometimes experience a warm, aching sensation which spreads from the needled point in various directions. This sensation was called *Têchi* by the Chinese; and the paths it traced – it often spreads a foot or more away from the site of the needle – could have been the starting point for a channel theory.

Dirty needles could have provided them with further evidence. The Chinese did not associate dirt with infection and certainly did not bother to sterilize their needles before sticking them into their next patient. Among other things, dirty needles can cause lymphangitis, an inflammation of the lymph vessels, which shows up as a red line from the wound to the nearest lymph node. Such lines can extend the whole length of a limb, from a toe to the groin or from a finger to the armpit.

Over the centuries Chinese acupuncturists could have collected many observations of *Têchi* and lymphangitis and built up a picture of a network of apparently interconnected channels. The principal objection to this explanation is that the meridians do not simply follow lymph vessels and do not invariably pass through lymph nodes.

Much more recently Dr Alex Macdonald, a Bristol doctor who gave up conventional general practice to devote himself to acupuncture, has come up with evidence which simultaneously explains meridians and knocks them firmly on the head. Dr Macdonald had long been puzzled as to why ancient Chinese textbooks illustrating meridians showed models posed in a variety of somewhat contrived positions. Unlike modern charts drawn up in the West which illustrate meridians by showing straightforward front and back views of the human body, the old Chinese books tended to select different poses for illustrating different meridians.

'It seemed as if the artist was actually drawing something he could see,' Dr Macdonald suggested. 'Sometimes the lines would be drawn firmly and clearly, at other times they would be more vague.'

He concluded that the artists had indeed been drawing what they saw and that the meridians were no more than a trick of the light.

While watching his two children playing in a paddling pool one day, Macdonald noticed that the bright sunlight reflected off their wet bodies in a tracery of highlights. As the children moved, reflections of light on their bodies traced the course of meridians illustrated in his Chinese textbook.

Macdonald decided to put this observation to the test. He hired a model and professional photographer. The model was covered in baby oil and posed in the same stances as those adopted by the textbook models. The flash lamp provided a single multidirectional source of light. Lo and behold, the meridians appeared on her skin almost identical to those shown in the old illustrations. On flatter areas of skin the light was rather diffused, but on strongly curved areas like the arm, leg, shoulder and face, the meridians shone out as clearly defined highlights.

If, like Macdonald, you reject the idea of Chi flowing along meridians, you still have to explain how a needle inserted at a particular spot can relieve pain or stimulate tissue on the other side or other end of the body. This is the most remarkable aspect of acupuncture and it is only partially explained by those who have turned away from classical theory. Why, for example, should an acupuncture point on the foot be used for treating a stiff neck or headache? The Chinese explained it by saying that the head and foot were connected by the gall bladder meridian. But if the meridian does not exist, what healing mechanism is at work?

Dr Felix Mann, the doyen of British medical acupuncturists, was one of the first British doctors to learn classical acupuncture thoroughly and practise it in this country. While he insists that the meridians are no more real than the geographical meridians on a map, he suggests that the phenomenon can be explained in terms of conventional, known physiology.

Physiologists with no interest in acupuncture have noticed that stimulation of the skin can produce changes in the heart and other viscera. Many such reflexes can be elicited by stimulating distant parts of the body which have no obvious connection with the site of the reflex. What the Chinese regarded as channels, Dr Mann believes to be a chain of visceral, cutaneous and nervous reflexes.

Reflexes of this kind might play a part in that other much observed but poorly understood phenomenon – trigger points. Trigger points are small areas on the surface of the body which become spontaneously tender during particular kinds of disease. People with heart disease, for instance, often manifest trigger points in the shoulder, chest and arm. One of the best-known trigger points, which occurs in acute appendicitis, is 'McBurney's point', a tender spot on the abdomen, which like all trigger points causes a jab of pain when it is prodded. Some trigger points are served by the same nerve pathway to the brain as the diseased organs, but sometimes they lie far away from any easily identifiable nervous connection.

The Canadian pain researcher Professor Ronald Melzack has recently shown that there is a remarkably high correlation – 71 per cent to be exact – between trigger points and traditional acupuncture points used to relieve pain, and that they act in the same way. Although prodding a trigger point will cause pain, prolonged stimulation of that point by needles, electrodes or the injection of local anaesthetic will make the pain in the diseased organ subside.

Writing in the international medical journal *Pain* (February 1977) he concurred with conventional medical opinion by declaring acupuncture meridians 'anatomically non-existent'. But he added, 'it is reasonable to assume that acupuncture points for pain relief are derived from the same kind of empirical observation . . . pressure at certain points is associated with particular pain patterns, and brief, intense stimulation of the points by needling sometimes produces prolonged relief. These considerations suggest a hypothesis: that trigger points and acupuncture points for pain, though discovered independently and labelled differently, represent the same phenomenon.'

In other words, even if meridians do not exist, acupuncture points obviously do. British medical acupuncturists have found further physical evidence of acupuncture points. Felix

Mann finds that 'fibrositic modules' or small strips of tense muscle occur spontaneously at traditional acupuncture points and disappear when the disease goes. Like trigger points they may occur at some distance from any diseased organ.

The site and location of acupuncture points has also been investigated by measuring electrical activity in the skin. Dr Ann Woolley-Hart of St Bartholomew's Hospital, London, has found that the electrical resistance of the skin at traditional acupuncture points is low but returns to normal once the point has been stimulated with a needle.

She has also found that patients with liver disease have low resistance in the skin around the knee joint. Interestingly enough, traditional acupuncture cites two acupuncture points on the knee joint, both of which are on the liver meridian.

In 1975 the West German Professor Melhardt reported similar findings to the 20th International Congress on Acupuncture in Vienna. He had found that resistance of the skin was much lower in certain well-defined areas. By experimenting with electrodes of differing sizes he found that these points, which he called 'reaction points', were about 2 mm in diameter. Having charted all his reaction points he found that they coincided with traditional acupuncture points.

Many acupuncturists, both medical and lay, use electrodes to find the low resistance points and use electric needles for the acupuncture itself. Purists claim that these methods are both crude and unnecessary. And Dr Woolley-Hart, who is not an acupuncturist but a specialist in medical electronics, points out that the instruments used for finding acupuncture points need careful handling. Changes in resistance can be brought about by simply scratching the skin, and unless the researcher is very careful not to stroke or stimulate the skin before beginning his tests, he cannot be certain what he is measuring.

At the Vienna conference the French anatomist Professor Jacques Bossy reported that he had dissected 201 acupuncture points on post mortem corpses and amputated limbs, and had found that 58 of these points lay in cerebrospinal nerves, 69 were in the outer walls of major blood vessels and 74 were in what anatomists call neurovascular bundles, which are concentrations of nerve around a blood vessel. His findings have since been confirmed by the Chinese.

Writing in *World Medicine* (22 August 1973), the American physician Dr Jack Geiger, who was one of the first American doctors to visit China after the Cultural Revolution, reported that the Chinese had found that 'the most important of the traditional acupuncture points have been shown to lie above particularly heavy concentrations of proprioceptors in muscle and tendon tissue'. (Proprioceptors are nerves which relay information to the brain about the position and activity of the tissue in which they are sited.)

'Vigorous and prolonged massage and deep pressure on proprioceptors – in areas where this is anatomically possible, such as the traditional Ho-ku acupuncture point on the dorsal aspect of the hand between the bases of the thumb and index finger – will induce surgical anaesthesia . . . without the use of acupuncture needles,' Geiger reported. 'Presumably, then, either needling or deep massage can stimulate the necessary neurological discharge along proprioceptive pathways.'

What Geiger is in fact describing is a technique used by parents the world over since time immemorial. When a child hurts itself and runs screaming to its mother, the sensible parent – who doubtless knows nothing of proprioceptors and neurological discharges – will kiss the bruise, massage it vigorously, and utter the calming words: 'Let Mummy rub it better.' The Chinese have developed the Mummy-rub-it-better method into a sophisticated technique called Shiatsu, which is basically acupuncture without needles, relying on finger pressure on certain sites where nerves meet near the surface of the body.

A possible explanation for the pain-killing effects of acupuncture and the Mummy-rub-it-better method has been given by Professor Patrick Wall of London University and Professor Ronald Melzack of McGill University in Canada. Wall and Melzack's theory, which is widely accepted by doctors specializing in pain control, is that a hypothetical 'gate' in the spinal cord can prevent pain signals from reaching the brain.

Briefly, stimulation of certain small nerve fibres opens the gate, while stimulation of larger types of nerve fibre closes the gate. The intense pain caused by shingles, for instance, is believed to be the result of the disease's destruction of certain thick nerve fibres which normally have the effect of closing the gate. However, when what remains of those fibres is activated by an electrical stimulator or by massage, the pain abates, sometimes for weeks or months. Wall and Melzack suggest that the intense stimulation caused by acupuncture closes the gate and thereby anaesthetizes various areas of the body.

One of the most senational claims made for acupuncture in recent years is that it can be used to cure drug addicts of their addiction. Several practitioners in Britain, Hong Kong and the USA have reported modest success in this field. Their method usually consists of putting a staple in the patient's ear lobe – a kind of permanent acupuncture. No one is sure why this should work, though recent research by biochemists investigating the chemistry of pain has suggested that there could be a link between addiction and pain mechanisms.

It has recently been found that the body reacts to pain by producing substances known as endorphins. Endorphins are not similar chemically to opiate drugs (eg morphine, heroin), but they stimulate the same cells and act on the body in a similar fashion. Heroin addicts have lower than average levels of endorphin in their spinal fluid. Acupuncture, however, invariably raises endorphin levels if the needles are left in for long enough. Moreover, the anti-narcotic drug naloxone, which is used to reverse the effects of opiates, can also abolish analgesia induced by acupuncture.

The pain-killing effects of acupuncture cannot all be explained chemically, however. Very often painful conditions can be relieved almost instantaneously by acupuncture. This effect can hardly be credited to endorphin which only reaches significantly higher levels in the spinal fluid after about 20 minutes of needling.

Alex Macdonald stresses that one should not confuse acupuncture *treatment* with acupuncture *analgesia*. The latter, which is often wrongly called acupuncture 'anaesthesia', refers to the use of needles for making a particular spot less sensitive to pain – as a preliminary to surgery, for instance. In acupuncture treatment the aim is not to make the spot numb but to remove the cause of pain.

As I mentioned earlier, Macdonald eschews all belief in meridians. When he examines patients he looks for small areas of muscle spasm. These spots occur spontaneously in painful illnesses and are distributed in unique patterns for each patient. Muscle spasm, he suggests, is the body's natural reaction to a noxious stimulus. If you put your hand on a hot stove, you withdraw it quickly and instinctively. Noxious stimuli always prompt this kind of reflex withdrawal. The system works perfectly when you want to avoid unpleasant external stimuli like hot stoves. But when the stimulus comes from inside the body itself – from a swollen joint, for example – the body ends up trying to withdraw from part of itself. The brain, which has a vested interest in trying to keep the body in one piece, tries to modify this reflex movement, and the muscles caught in the resulting nervous crossfire go into spasm.

The situation can be remedied, Macdonald suggests, by applying another noxious stimulus like a needle (though it could equally well be a cold pack, small electric shock, heat or even a nettle sting) to another site. If the acupuncturist chooses his site correctly the original noxious reflex will be cancelled out by the body withdrawing from the new stimulus.

A large proportion of Macdonald's patients suffer from rheumatoid or osteo-arthritis, common complaints whose symptoms are usually pain and stiffness. The stiffness, he believes, is largely the result of muscular malfunction. Pain, however, is an emotional reaction. The brain not only commands limbs to move but also predicts the sensation it will receive from muscles and joints when that movement is carried out correctly. When a patient is in chronic pain, abnormal reflex patterns cause muscles to go into spasm. These abnormal reflex patterns prevent the brain's commands from being carried out, and abnormal movements occur. The sensations of these do not match those the brain is expecting to receive. And this mismatch between what is expected and what is happening generates the emotion of pain.

The idea that pain is an emotion rather than a pure sensation like sight, smell or touch is not unique to Macdonald, but it is a quite modern idea. The old classical theory of pain put forward by medical theorists was that certain nerves were pain nerves, which picked up information about physical damage and relayed this information directly to the brain. Impulses from the pain nerves would activate pain cells in the brain, and when this happened we would agonize accordingly. Anatomists have now shown that this old theory, despite its attractive simplicity, is quite wrong; there are neither pain nerves nor pain cells. The perception of pain is modified and controlled at several stages in the nervous system. It is usually set off by some kind of damage to tissue, but the intensity of pain experienced by the sufferer depends on a number of things, notably mood. Anxiety is known to increase pain, and people who have suffered chronic pain for years due to disease may still go on suffering even when the original cause of that pain has gone. Conversely, pain can disappear when the patient is hypnotized, elated or simply has his or her attention directed elsewhere.

Needles inserted through the skin will also produce reflex patterns via the spinal cord. These patterns can counteract those which were responsible for pain. The needle could be inserted in any of a number of spots to achieve this effect, though Macdonald generally slips a needle into the skin overlying an area of muscle spasm. Sometimes a needle inserted into an area like the heel, where there is no muscle, will nevertheless produce a strong enough stimulus to counteract a headache or backache.

If all the modern theories outlined are at least partially correct, there are obviously a number of mechanisms at work in acupuncture. On the one hand, prolonged stimulation makes the body produce its own natural pain-killing substances, the endorphins. Alternatively, or even simultaneously, the needles are causing reflexes which improve muscle tone. Then again, vigorous twiddling of the needles could be stimulating thick nerve fibres to close that pain 'gate' and thus prevent unpleasant messages from reaching the brain.

It is still difficult to explain why a needle inserted in, say, the right pectoral major muscle in the chest should be able to relieve pain in the left knee. We have the analogy of the trigger points, those tender spots which arise far from the site of the diseased organ; but no one has yet explained just what causes trigger points.

Another British general practitioner who specializes in acupuncture, Julian Kenyon, prefers Robert Becker's explanation that acupuncture works by activating electrical pathways. These pathways, he suggests, run through the neuroglia, the connective tissue of the nervous system. Twiddling the needle produces a direct current which is conducted through the neuroglia to a distant site. This explains how a needle in the right part of the chest can treat a pain in the left knee, or how a needle inserted at the traditional acupuncture point 'Liver 3', which is sited near the big toe, can cure a migraine.

Kenyon does not deny the existence of the muscle spasms described by Macdonald, nor of the nodules described by Felix Mann; but he finds that the needle at Liver 3 will get rid of the migraine whether or not there happens to be a spasm or nodule on that spot.

It is often suggested that acupuncture really works through some form of hypnosis. Hypnosis certainly can abolish pain, but there are major differences between the analgesia induced by each technique. Firstly, patients can be hypnotized in 60 seconds and successfully undergo surgery without pain-killing drugs. To achieve that kind of analgesia with acupuncture takes about 30 minutes of twiddling or electrical stimulation through the needles. Moreover, acupuncture analgesia can be blocked by giving the patient that opiate antagonist drug, naloxone. Hypnotic analgesia is not affected by naloxone. Thirdly, animal experiments have shown that acupuncture analgesia is abolished if the dorsolateral tract in the spinal cord is cut. This effect does not occur with hypnotized animals.

Another controversy which obscures understanding of acupuncture analgesia centres on how well the acupuncturist can localize the analgesia he induces. In the August 1977 issue of the journal *Pain* Drs Lynn and Perl, researchers at North Carolina University, reported that although experienced acupuncturists under their surveillance had been able to raise the pain thresholds of volunteers, this effect had not consistently occurred in the areas predicted by the acupuncturists. Before they inserted their needles the acupuncturists were asked to tell the investigators which areas they intended to make numb. Sometimes they were on target, but just as often they were way off beam; and there was no significant evidence to prove that they had any really accurate notion of what areas they would affect.

Demonstrations by individual practitioners have shown that this is not always the case, however. Dr Robert Graham, a British general practitioner who lives in County Durham, showed how it could be done at the scientific meeting of the American Society of Clinical Hypnosis in 1972. He rendered the upper jaw of a Mississippi dentist, Dr J. C. Shirley, completely numb by inserting two needles in classical acupuncture points between the thumb and forefinger and twirling them for 15 minutes. Dr Graham had been greeted with scepticism when he claimed that he could make the upper jaw numb without affecting sensation in the lower jaw. In the event, the gum of his volunteer's upper jaw was probed until it bled without him feeling a thing. When his lower jaw was probed, he felt acute pain.

Sometimes quasi-hypnotic influences do have an effect on analgesia. The Finnish professor of anaesthesia, Dr Pekka Pöntinen, discovered that he could use the same acupuncture points to induce analgesia in patients who were either going to have their tonsils out or who were going to have teeth extracted. When it came to the operation, though, he found that the patients who were expecting to have their tonsils out were hypersensitive to pain in their teeth, while the patients who were waiting to have their teeth extracted could not bear to be touched on the tonsils! It seems that the patient's expectations must play some part in the success or failure of acupuncture.

One of the first things Chinese doctors proudly showed Western medical men when the country opened its doors to visitors in the early 1970s was patients undergoing complicated surgery with little but acupuncture to stop the pain. Small amounts of analgesic drugs were sometimes given too, however. Since then the Chinese have surveyed 80,000 operations in which the patient was given acupuncture. Only 37 per cent responded strongly enough to feel no pain. A further 38 per cent experienced slight pain and emitted the occasional groan. Only one patient in twelve responded so poorly that he had to be given a general anaesthetic.

Another reason Chinese patients might be more prepared to do without drugs is that anaesthetic standards in China are much lower than in the West. Many more patients are thought to die under anaesthesia in China than they do in British and American hospitals. So there could be rather more incentive to opt for the safer procedure.

Most British medical acupuncturists believe that acupuncture can only be of limited use in the operating theatre. When Dr Felix Mann conducted a series of 100 experiments (reported in the *British Journal of Anaesthesia* in 1974), he found that analgesia was only just strong enough for the patients to undergo surgery in ten per cent of cases. In 65 per cent he was able to induce mild analgesia but certainly not enough to obliterate the pain of an operation.

Since completing that trial he has come to the conclusion that only one person in twenty reacts strongly enough to acupuncture for it to be an effective surgical analgesic. Other practitioners find this figure far too pessimistic, but even they admit that acupuncture is a cumbersome procedure in comparison with conventional drug methods. Dr Robert Graham offered his services to a dentist to see if acupuncture would be a viable alternative to local anaesthetics for fillings and extractions. He had little problem making the patients' jaws analgesic, but he had to spend 20 minutes with each of them to do it. The dentist pointed out that acupuncture was all very well, but that if he had to rely on that alone he would only be able to treat half as many patients in a day.

Most of the patients who go to medical acupuncturists are suffering from painful conditions, and the doctors report 70 per cent success in treating arthritis, migraine, sinusitis and period pains. Their success with back pain is variable but seems to compare very well with conventional orthopaedic or drug treatments. Asthma responds well too, as do a number of psychosomatic complaints, although it is difficult to explain why.

Acupuncture does *not* help with diseases which have resulted in actual destruction of tissue. It may relieve the pain of angina or cancer, but it does not cure the disease. In fact, acupuncture's great ability to relieve pain is a potential hazard unless the acupuncturist is a skilled diagnostician. The main objection medical acupuncturists have to unqualified practitioners of the therapy is that the layman can successfully mask a dangerous disease by blotting out its symptoms.

Lay acupuncturists vary considerably in their medical knowledge. Some have been trained at osteopathic colleges and do at least have a background in anatomy and physiology. Others do not. Most lay acupuncturists diagnose and assess the progress of disease in the traditional Chinese manner (or what they believe to be the traditional Chinese manner). Like the ancient Chinese acupuncturists they claim they can predict future diseases to which the patient is likely to succumb. Patients are told that if they want to prevent themselves falling victim to some future ill, they should come in for regular treatment. It is of course quite reasonable to predict that a person who lives a stressful life, who smokes, drinks and who has a poor diet, will fall grievously ill before long. But acupuncture will not stop that happening. Only a change of habits will do any good. Regular treatment only keeps the acupuncturist's bank account healthy.

Some lay acupuncturists tell their patients to give up all their prescribed drugs, before commencing treatment. In fact, acupuncture has no known effect on the way the body metabolizes drugs. Some doctors have found that acupuncture may not work as efficiently for patients who are on steroids, strong tranquillizers, antidepressants, or the ergotamine drugs used to treat migraine. Sometimes patients who have had electroconvulsive therapy (ECT) hardly respond to acupuncture. In an ideal world it would be wonderful if nobody took drugs; nevertheless, the effects of sudden withdrawal from drugs can be catastrophic, and most lay acupuncturists do not have enough knowledge of drugs to know whether withdrawal will help the patient or harm him.

Possibly the most worrying aspect of acupuncture in untrained hands is the real damage which can be done. Most medical acupuncturists use short needles about an inch long and 32 mm in diameter. They are sterilized or disposable. The more ambitious among the lay fraternity may use needles a foot long which are plunged deep into the body.

Acupuncture needles rarely cause damage to tissue. They divide rather than tear and can even pass through a major artery without causing a haemorrhage. But if a long needle is being used, accuracy is essential. In Sweden four deaths were reported as resulting from the needle being inserted into the chest just ten degrees out of its correct trajectory. Collapsed lungs have been the result of accidents in at least one British hospital.

If the lay acupuncturist adopts the traditional Chinese approach to hygiene and does not bother to sterilize his needles, the patient may get hepatitis. This has already happened at least twice in Britain.

Any unqualified person can practise acupuncture in Britain as long as he does not claim to be a registered medical practitioner. The Acupuncture Association represents lay acupuncturists, most of whom are osteopaths or naturopaths and some of whom have attended the short courses offered to foreigners in Taiwan. Membership of the Acupuncture

3

Association may indicate that the practitioner is not totally devoid of basic medical knowledge, but patients should not be misled by the title 'Doctor of Acupuncture' which is sported by some of its members. These doctorates are not recognized by any body other than the Acupuncture Association. Doctorates and even 'professorships' are also conferred by institutions in Taiwan and Hong Kong, but they are not recognized by British universities. Perhaps they should just call themselves 'qualified acupuncturists' – Qu Acs – and have done with it.

Some British doctors who practise acupuncture have been to The People's Republic of China to learn how modern acupuncture is practised there. This is true of few, if any, non-medically qualified acupuncturists. Mainland Chinese universities do not award doctorates in acupuncture to foreigners who spend a few weeks in the country. Indeed the Peking government's policy is to replace traditionally trained lay acupuncturists by qualified doctors who have been trained in basic medicine as well as acupuncture.

One cannot be hard on the lay acupuncturists without pointing out that some properly qualified doctors who claim to practise acupuncture have precious little idea of what they are doing, except that they recognize a profitable bandwagon when they see one.

The Medical Acupuncture Association, whose founder and president is Dr Felix Mann, runs courses for doctors, which are highly respected, although brief. Unlike the Acupuncture Association, which is keen on publicity, the Medical Acupuncture Association shuns it. This is probably due as much to ethical considerations as to the fact that some of its members are in private practice and could easily be accused of drawing financial advantage from publicity – which could result in their being struck off the Medical Register.

Unfortunately acupuncture does not fit in easily with the conventional pattern of general practice. A few GPs like Dr Graham manage to combine the two, but many GPs have had to give up their NHS practice because acupuncture takes up more than the six minutes the NHS GP can afford to spend on each patient.

In France about 1500 doctors use acupuncture, and ten French hospitals have departments of acupuncture. It is taught in Russian medical schools. In the United Kingdom only about 70 doctors belong to the Medical Acupuncture Association and the technique is not taught in medical schools despite its obvious potential in the treatment of chronic disease.

8 Manipulation—Bones of Contention

> Most doctors working in casualty departments claim to have seen the ill effects of osteopathy. But they rarely bother to find out whether it was a registered osteopath who did the damage, or whether it was an untrained person just calling himself an osteopath.

That complaint comes not, as you might expect, from a registered osteopath but from a doctor, John Ebbetts. As president of an organization with an aptly onomatopoeic title, BAMM (the British Association for Manipulative Medicine), Dr Ebbetts is one of a minority of doctors who have been trying for decades to have manipulation brought into the syllabus of medical education. Their cause has not been helped by the activities of unqualified bonesetters nor by the claims and theories of the osteopathic and chiropractic professions which medics have traditionally dismissed as unproven, if not downright ludicrous.

Dr Ebbetts cites a classic example of the quack osteopath. A patient of his was a part-time coal merchant. When trade was slack in the summer he set up in business with his girlfriend as a clairvoyant in Brighton. This clairvoyant coalman visited Dr Ebbetts six times as a patient complaining of a slipped disc. He insisted that his girl-friend should attend every consultation with him 'to complete the vibrations'.

After six sessions he still complained of backache, though Dr Ebbetts had been through every relevant diagnostic and therapeutic procedure, and could find nothing wrong. Bills for treatment were sent but never paid. Two months later Dr Ebbetts noticed an advertisement in the local paper for 'osteopathic treatment'. The advertiser was none other than the clairvoyant coalman. His total knowledge of manipulation had apparently been gathered from the observations his girlfriend had made during those six consultations.

Dr Ebbetts was not particularly worried about the possible harm the charlatan could have wrought. Manipulation, he says, is a reasonably safe activity as long as the practitioner does not get over-ambitious and try to bend something further than nature intended. If the coalman could successfully run a clairvoyant business for holiday-makers, he doubtless had the gift of the gab. 'I expect that he was charming and listened to his patients and gave them the kind of attention a doctor has not got time for. I imagine he had a lot of satisfied patients.'

Not all medically trained manipulators and osteopaths are so optimistic, however. Anyone can call himself an osteopath and even purport to hold a diploma in osteopathy without breaking the law, and hundreds of people are doing just that. Estimates vary considerably, but there are now believed to be something between 500 and 3000 unqualified people practising under the title of osteopath, chiropractor, 'physiologist', 'reflexotherapist' and other styles. And they are catering for a booming market. In 1975 Department of Health statistics showed that back pain of various sorts was losing the country over 13 million working days a year. Dr Ebbetts suggests that at least a million manipulations are performed every week. Only a tiny proportion of those are done by medically qualified manipulators. Apart from a minority of patients who mistrust medics and avoid them on principle, almost every patient who seeks osteopathic or chiropractic treatment has been failed by their GP or terrified by the prospect of orthopaedic surgery. The lay manipulators cater for them, though only a few hundred have had any formal training at all.

In 1867 the surgeon Sir James Paget issued this warning to young doctors: 'Few of you are likely to practise without having a bone-setter for a rival; and if he can cure a case which you have failed to cure, his fortune will be made, and yours marred.'

His warning has gone unheeded. The British Association for Manipulative Medicine, which unites doctors representing the whole range of manipulative theories and techniques, has only about 300 members. (There are over 50,000 doctors in the UK, more than half of them general practitioners who see cases of backache every working day.)

A hundred and ten years after Sir James Paget's warning, Dr James Cyriax wrote these words in *General Practitioner*:

The reason why manipulation, especially spinal, lies under a cloud today is not that it is ineffective – everyone knows of cases where it was dramatically successful – but that it is carried out by people of whom doctors disapprove.

Medical prejudice is understandable, for many of these laymen profess a dogma that those with a scientific training cannot accept, and attribute symptoms to wholly imaginary lesions.

This does not imply, however, that lay *practice* can be rejected with the same ease as lay theories. Manipulation, especially spinal, is often successful even when based on a faulty idea of where the fault lies.

It hardly matters what these men think; what matters is what they do, and it is up to medical men not to deride their failures but to study their successes.

Dr Cyriax, author of *The Slipped Disc* and former consultant orthopaedic physician at St Thomas's Hospital in London, has been the scourge of lay manipulators for forty years and has consistently called for manipulation to be brought into the medical fold. He has also had unkind words to say about orthopaedic surgeons with their slap-happy love of the knife; nor has he endeared himself to the few doctors who practise osteopathy and report equal success to his own.

The principal objection most medics have to osteopaths and chiropractors is that they claim to cure much more than back and joint problems. In Britain most of them do confine themselves to spinal problems, largely because these are the problems which most of their patients come to them with. In the United States and Canada where chiropractors have been licensed to practise in some states and provinces, they tend to be more ambitious in their claims. Diabetes, cancer, epilepsy and anaemia are curable by chiropractic according to pamphlets and advertisements published in recent years.

When Dr Norman Shealy (Chapter Six) organized a medical conference in Wisconsin in 1974 to discuss both conventional and unconventional approaches to the treatment of chronic pain, he invited clairvoyants, healers and a man who diagnoses illness by receiving mediumistic communications through a harp, as well as local surgeons and physicians. His medical colleagues had no objection to the psychics, nor even to the harp therapist, but were furious to learn that he had asked a chiropractor to come too.

Osteopaths in the United States, on the other hand, are regarded as being on equal terms with doctors. The doctorate in osteopathy has equivalent status to the MD degree, and osteopaths are employed as doctors in government institutions and the armed forces. This is due to the fact that American osteopathic schools now teach a syllabus which is almost indistinguishable from that of a medical school. Manipulation is now regarded as no more important than conventional therapeutics. There are even osteopathic surgeons, something quite unheard of in Britain.

It is also something which would make Andrew Taylor Still, the founder of osteopathy, turn in his grave. Still, who was born in 1828, was the son of a Middle Western Methodist preacher and hand healer. In his own writings he declares that osteopathy was revealed to him by God in 1874. He had in fact begun to rail against the inadequacies and dangers of contemporary medicine ten years earlier after his three children had died of meningitis. He had helped his father minister to native Indian folk, and it is possible that he picked up some bone-setting techniques from them and from some of the newly arrived immigrants from Europe.

His resentment at the conventional medicine of the day, which was doubtless extremely primitive in his part of the United States, prompted him to develop manipulation into a holistic alternative. He concluded that dislocated bones, especially in the back, associated with muscle spasm and weakened ligaments were the root of most, if not all, disease.

Dislocations, he averred, put pressure on blood vessels and nerves, which consequently prevented the natural flow of life forces to other parts of the body. God had designed the body perfectly, he believed, and the body should therefore be able to throw off any disease, provided it was in good mechanical order.

Although his knowledge of anatomy was wildly inaccurate, this holistic approach would have been reasonable enough. The trouble was that Still thought manipulation was the only way to set wrongs right. He did recommend the medical virtue of some foods, especially honey, but claimed among other things that goitre was caused by 'slipping of the first rib', that constipation could be relieved by manipulating the atlas (the uppermost segment of the spine) and that the use of nappies could dislocate babies' hips, which would subsequently lead to diabetes.

Still could be dismissed as a crank and a liar; but even if he did cure people of so many complaints, it can hardly have been as a result of his manipulations. A more credible, though no less remarkable, explanation might be that he had inherited some of his father's hand healing ability, and that unbeknown to himself he was using the kind of 'energy' described in Chapter One.

Daniel David Palmer, an Iowa grocer, was the founder of chiropractic. He drew his inspiration from a number of sources, one of which may have been a pupil from the osteopathic school Still had founded in Kirksville, Missouri, in 1892. Before alighting on his manipulative therapy, he had worked as a 'magnetic healer'. His first patient was his janitor, who told Palmer that he had gone stone deaf after dislocating his neck. Palmer corrected the dislocation – apparently more by instinct than education – and the man's hearing was restored.

Palmer evolved a theory that disease was the result of the pressure of dislocated bones on nerves and that this interference would upset the function of all organs.

It is unfair to dwell too much on the history of osteopathy

and chiropractic, replete as they are with colourful characters, dubious educational institutions and get-rich-quick schemes. The American medical profession was full of chancers, incompetents and rogues during that expansive phase of the country's history. And even today there are probably more surgeons in the United States who perform unnecessary operations to line their pockets than there are chiropractors who claim to cure all manner of ills by manipulation. It is largely because the medical profession has failed to put its own house in order that heterodox practitioners have attracted popular support.

To the outsider the difference between modern osteopathic practice and chiropractic are minimal. In very broad terms osteopaths tend to use leverage, rotating and lifting on the patient, whereas chiropractors go in for well directed thrusts at particular vertebrae. Techniques do overlap considerably, however, and some manipulators actually prefer to use the term 'osteopractic'.

Osteopaths and chiropractors claim that the main difference between their kind of therapy and that promoted by Dr Cyriax is that their methods cause the patient much less pain. Cyriax retorts that many of the lesions which osteopaths and chiropractors claim to cure do not exist.

Dr Cyriax suggests that the only reason to manipulate the spine is to replace a slipped disc. The discs are the fibrous pads between each vertebra, which act as shock absorbers. The discs are filled with a jelly-like substance, which can bulge through the fibrous outer layer of the disc if it is subject to heavy strain. The bulge can press on spinal nerves, nerve roots or the spinal cord itself and thus cause pain. If the bulge is large it may be impossible and dangerous to try and manipulate it back into place. In such cases traction is used so that the spine is stretched and the protruding piece of disc can slip back into place.

When a faulty spine is successfully manipulated a distinct 'click' is often heard. The old osteopathic explanation for this was that the displaced vertebra was falling back into its correct position. The discovery and use of X-rays has shown that this is not the case. Dr Cyriax argues that it is the movement of the disc fragment which causes the click. Most osteopaths suggest that it results from the breakdown of adhesions which have built up in spinal joints and prevented movement. Neither explanation can be proven, however, and this lack of conclusive evidence has allowed the acrimonious dispute between the rival parties to smoulder on for decades.

The Cyriax school of thought insists that manipulation is only good for problems like back pain, sciatica and lumbago which are caused by derangements of the disc. Osteopaths and chiropractors go much further; they believe that spinal problems can upset organs far away.

A flat foot, for instance, makes one leg shorter than the other; this leads to abnormal curvature of the spine. The head is tilted to one side, muscles contract to keep it level, and tension ensues, giving the patient a headache. Other organic problems, they believe, can be brought on indirectly by spasm in the muscles caused by a malfunctioning joint. The idea, briefly, is that the lesion unnaturally stimulates the autonomic nervous system, which is responsible for the proper functioning of the heart, digestive system, and many other organs. This interference with normal function puts a stress on the whole system, which thus becomes more prone to breakdown.

Osteopathic and chiropractic literature in Britain does not suggest that manipulation can cure disease in organs once the tissue has been damaged, though it does claim that functional disorders can be checked if they are caught early enough.

Acupuncture has shown that correction of muscle spasm and stimulation of particular areas can cause changes far away in the body. Opinions differ as to why this should be. Likewise the osteopath's ideas, while perhaps not as wrong as some doctors claim, are not demonstrably right either.

Earlier in this chapter I suggested that Andrew Taylor Still may have succeeded with his patients because he had healing energy in his hands. A number of osteopaths believe that this could explain some of their successes too. Peter Blagrave, president of the Society of Osteopaths, told me that some of his patients seemed to benefit out of all proportion to the manipulation they had been given. And Dr John Lester, the former dean of the London College of Osteopathy, suggested that the results of osteopathy and hand healing were often indistinguishable.

Dr Lester works with healers and has great respect for their abilities. He was once keen to run clinical trials of osteopathy to collect hard statistics which might persuade sceptical medical colleagues that it was a successful technique. He is now convinced that any comparison made between the clinical competence of one practitioner to another would be a test of their natural healing powers as much as of their manipulative methods.

The chiropractor David Tansley has long given up spinal manipulation in favour of radionic healing directed at the 'chakras' – an Indian concept of vortices of energy situated down the spine.

Such notions are quite alien to the majority of manipulators. To understand the basis of Tansley's ideas one requires a knowledge of radiesthesia, Indian philosophy and mysticism which I do not have and which very few others would want to have. And even if senior osteopaths are prepared to admit that hand healing helps their patients, there is no sign of it being included in the osteopathic colleges' syllabus.

But as Dr Cyriax pointed out: 'It hardly matters what these men think; what matters is what they do.' That is certainly the patients' attitude too. People go to osteopaths and chiropractors because they cannot get help elsewhere, and they pay for their treatment in cash.

Nobody really knows how successful their treatment is. One medically qualified osteopath declared that he cured 90 per cent of his patients with backache; Dr Cyriax reports that one of his registrars who later trained and practised as a medical osteopath managed to cure only ten per cent. A survey carried out by the Osteopathic Association of Great Britain in 1977 reported that its members claimed the 'expected improvement' in 73.7 per cent of the patients they treated, and 'more than expected improvement' in another 9.1 per cent. However successful they are, we should remember that almost all their

154

patients have been doctors' failures.

It is interesting that the British Association of Manipulative Medicine should have elected to base the courses it runs for doctors on osteopathic techniques of manipulation. As far as diagnosis is concerned, it recommends a mixture of the methods used by osteopaths and those employed by Dr Cyriax. BAMM's courses are short, lasting just four weekends, and are intended to give practising doctors a few basic manipulations which will help them deal with the common back problems encountered in a GP's surgery.

Manipulative medicine is taught to students at St Thomas's Hospital medical school, but, as far as I know, at no other medical school as yet. The other institution which teaches doctors manipulation is the London College of Osteopathy. It has about 50 graduates, who can put the letters LLCO after their name, but it seems to have run out of steam recently, and its courses have been suspended.

Doctors who have bothered to take a look at the colleges which train lay osteopaths and chiropractors have been pleasantly surprised by the teaching standards. Dr Philip Wood, who is on the staff of the Arthritis and Rheumatism Council, said that he had found the British School of Osteopathy and the Anglo-European College of Chiropractic 'surprisingly good'. As well as these two colleges there are the British College of Naturopathy and Osteopathy in Hampstead and the European College of Osteopathy, in Maidstone, Kent. Dr Ebbetts points out that the major disadvantage suffered by students at these colleges is that they cannot dissect corpses like medical students – 'and that is the only really satisfactory way to learn anatomy'. But in radiology he believes that chiropractors especially have the edge on most doctors.

Radiology is an important tool for the manipulator. X-rays can help determine whether there is cancer or other bone diseases in the spine which would make manipulation hazardous. Although no unqualified bone-setter has yet been sued for destroying a patient by manipulting a tuberculous or cancerous spine, it could be only a matter of time before this happens. Fortunately TB of the spine is a rare disease in Britain.

Dr John Lester, however, believes that the often repeated warnings about the dangers of manipulation are 'a big red herring'. He has treated patients with secondary tumours: 'I do not manipulate, but I articulate the joint and strap it, which lets the patient die in comfort.'

The main problem for anyone who seeks the services of an osteopath or chiropractor is to sort out one who has been trained. Fringe practitioners sport all kind of strange letters after their names which mean nothing to the uninitiated. The British School of Osteopathy and the European College award the diploma 'DO'. Graduates of the Naturopathic and Osteopathic College style themselves 'DO. ND'. The Anglo-European College of Chiropractic, which is conveniently situated in Bournemouth where it can attract students from France where such pursuits are illegal, awards a doctorate, 'DC'.

The trouble is that you, me or anyone else can put these letters behind our names if we feel so inclined, and nobody can do anything to stop us. In 1936 the General Council and Register of Osteopaths, which operates from the same address in London SW1 as the British School of Osteopathy, was set up at the suggestion of the then Minister of Health in an attempt to regulate the profession. Osteopaths who are on the Register can put the initials MRO after their names. Anyone who used these letters without being a member of the register could be successfully prosecuted by the Council.

However, the Council only recognizes graduates of the British School and the London College of Osteopathy. Its secretary explained that it would be prepared to consider graduates from the other schools if the schools allowed themselves to be inspected and their standards assessed by Council members. But the other schools have evinced no desire to be inspected and assessed.

The Society of Osteopaths accepts graduates from all four osteopathic colleges, who can then put the letters 'MSO' after their names. But here too we learn of schism and dissent. Some of the leading members and founders of the Society of Osteopaths once taught at the College of Naturopathy and

Osteopathy and decamped to the European College in Maidstone.

These squabbles have not helped the osteopaths to present a united front against totally unqualified practitioners. In 1976 Joyce Butler MP (known to her colleagues as the patron saint of lost causes) introduced a Private Member's Bill which was intended to make proper training and registration compulsory for osteopaths. The British School of Osteopathy and the General Council claim that they were not consulted at all on the drafting of the Bill and suspected that it would have obliged the Register to accept graduates from other schools willy nilly. In the event they did not have to worry long. The Bill failed for lack of parliamentary time.

It might seem a good idea to have osteopaths and chiropractors brought into the National Health Service where their services could be available to those hundreds of thousands of workers with back pains. Vague attempts have been made to do this, but they inevitably collapse. Firstly osteopaths and chiropractors are used to working independently and would not take kindly to being in a subordinate position like physiotherapists, who take their instructions from a doctor. Secondly, doctors might find it hard to agree with osteopathic and chiropractic diagnoses. Thirdly, patients have already shown that they are happy to spend their own money for private manipulation. And the Government is quite happy to let them pay for it.

The therapies we have looked at so far could be brought under a general heading of 'mainstream unorthodox'. Some are more widely practised than others, and some have attracted more serious scientific assessment than others, but they all fall neatly into the category of alternative medicine. and they are quite freely available to any patient who is prepared to take the risk.

The next chapters dwell on the subject of reincarnation, which may not immediately strike you as a medical matter at all. However the bulk of what I report is based on the studies and experiences of psychiatrists who are not only convinced that reincarnation is feasible, but also that traumas from a previous life impinge violently on one's mind and body in subsequent reincarnations.

The activities of Philippino psychic surgeons are included for reasons which will be explained, although much of what they do is highly suspect – though none the less worthy of serious investigation for all that. The psychiatrists are very different; by stating publicly what they believed, they had much to lose and little but notoriety to gain.

9 *Psychic Healing—Catharsis*

Dr Arthur Guirdham is blessed with two remarkable characteristics. Firstly he is the only psychiatrist in Somerset who claims to be a reincarnation of a Cathar priest from thirteenth-century Languedoc. Secondly, his physical appearance and his personality are the complete antithesis of what one would expect of a person who made such claims.

Perhaps my own experience and prejudices are not universal, but I tend to associate reincarnation with straggle-haired ladies in flowery dresses who fix you with a manic eye and assure you that once they were Cleopatra.

Dr Guirdham is not like that at all. He is a stocky, portly gentleman with a great bald dome and Roman nose, whose conversation is deliberate, down to earth and seasoned with irony. A nineteenth-century Englishman, whose virtues would have been admired by Dickens and Trollope, he is, above all, believable.

Dr Guirdham's believability has stood him in good stead. Without his solid roast beef qualities he would certainly have been dismissed as a crank. In fact he is a popular lecturer in Britain; a willing publisher has published eight of his books; and his articles on reincarnation and psychic healing are eagerly printed by the editors of medical magazines.

As it has already taken Dr Guirdham the space of several volumes to tell the full story of how he came to believe in reincarnation and psychic healing, I shall have to present a brief synopsis which lacks much of the convincing detail reported in the doctor's own books. Briefly though, the story runs thus.

Dr Guirdham qualified as a doctor in the 1920s and decided to specialize in psychiatry. He was awarded a research degree for a thesis he presented on the Rorschach test and as a young man won a number of prizes for further research work. By 1968, when he was forced to retire after suffering two coronaries, he was senior consultant psychiatrist in the Bath NHS area, psychiatrist to the Bath child guidance clinic and medical superintendent of a private mental hospital. In short, he was a highly competent doctor much respected by his colleagues. He had never evinced much liking for the occult or psychic phenomena and assures me that he has never attended a seance, consulted a medium or as much as visited a clairvoyant on Brighton pier before or since his 'conversion' to reincarnation and psychic healing. The only intimations of the revelation to come were a number of recurrent dreams which he had experienced for many years and whose significance he only understood later.

Unlike some addicts of reincarnation whose previous lives were invariably those of exalted personages and who only have to pass through the village of Fotheringhay to be seized by the certainty that they were once Mary Queen of Scots, Dr Guirdham claims a mundane initiation into his previous lives. It all began in his outpatients clinic in 1962.

A woman in her thirties, whom he calls 'Mrs Smith', had been referred to him by a general practitioner. She was not severely ill. Her GP did not believe she was psychotic or schizophrenic, but she was suffering from a mild anxiety. She had particularly asked to be referred to Dr Guirdham 'because of a dream she had had'. In the dream, which had recurred for many years and from which she always awoke screaming, she found herself in a large room. At the climax of the dream a sinister figure entered the room from the right. This nightmare struck a chord in Dr Guirdham. He had been having the same dream himself for many years. The only difference was that in his dream someone entered the room from the left.

After their first meeting neither of them had the dream again.

Mrs Smith's revelations did not stop there. She told Dr Guirdham that she had had many more dreams, and visions and 'memories' during her waking hours, in which she found herself in medieval Languedoc in the South of France. She was a member of the Cathar sect, a heretical movement which was savagely put down by the Inquisition in the thirteenth century. She claimed that she had been burnt at the stake. More remarkable still, she averred that Dr Guirdham had been her friend at this time and had also been arrested for heresy.

A sceptic with just a little knowledge of psychoanalysis may immediately assume that Mrs Smith was indulging in 'transference', a phenomenon often noted by analysts, in which the patient projects emotions on to the doctor which should properly be directed at her father, husband or other close relation who has been the origin of her neurosis. Others might suggest that she was doing what many women have done through the ages – that she had simply fallen in love with her doctor and developed a bizarre means of expressing this feeling.

Dr Guirdham chose not to accept this explanation, however. For as well as suggesting that he was her companion in a previous existence, Mrs Smith recounted a wealth of historical detail about the life of the Cathars in thirteenth-century France. She gave Guirdham a list of names and the detailed family background of members of Provençal squirearchy. Most of these 'memories' had come to her when she was a child in her teens. But meeting the doctor had opened the floodgates to further recollections.

None of the individuals she mentioned were at all well known historically; indeed none of their names had appeared in any published text. and certainly not in English translation. Guirdham subsequently checked all these names and all the other material provided by Mrs Smith with the two leading French authorities on Catharism – which is itself a backwater of French religious history – and they confirmed everything to the smallest detail. Many of the names and day-to-day trivia related by Mrs Smith could only be confirmed by the scholars' recourse to dog Latin transcripts made of Inquisition hearings which were only translated into French several months after Mrs Smith had reported them to Guirdham.

All in all, the lady was presenting a pretty good case for re-incarnation.

The revelations did not stop with Mrs Smith. Several other individuals, most of them women, but of no particular age group or common background except that they lived in or near Bath, provided Guirdham with more details about his and their lives as Cathars in Languedoc. One of the most remarkable, a lady whom the doctor calls Mrs Mills, seemed to arrive in his life by sheerest coincidence. She came to his door one day asking if she could use the telephone because her car had broken down on the road outside.

Not long afterwards she began to hear a discarnate female voice which dictated messages and names which she could not understand. She reported these messages to Guirdham, who found that they all related to the same thirteenth-century Cathar society.

Eventually 'the voice' materialized as a full blown vision of an old lady dressed in the blue robes of a Cathar priestess, wearing an ornate cross suspended from a girdle round her waist. This old lady, with her wrinkled, benign face, gave her name as Braïda and was subsequently to play a large part in Guirdham's experiences of psychic healing.

What I have related is the barest sketch of the events which convinced Dr Guirdham of reincarnation, and anyone who wants more thorough and convincing evidence must refer to the doctor's own writings. Reincarnation is in fact only the hors d'oeuvre to the main theme of this chapter, which is psychic healing.

From his experiences and observations Dr Guirdham has come to the conclusion that man is divided into three aspects: personality, psyche and individualized spirit. Personality is purely temporal; it is the creation of a person's lusts and emotions, the compromises between what you want to be and what society will let you be; it is the face a person presents to the world and 'riveted in time'. Psyche, he suggests, is largely emancipated from time and space; it is that part of the person which can drift from century to century or appear hundreds or thousands of miles away from the body as a discarnate entity.

Individualized spirit is totally emancipated from time and space and resembles what Christians call the Holy Spirit and Buddhists call the Common Ground.

Although Guirdham had been occupied with the personality for the greater part of his medical career, his later experiences and researches interested him increasingly in the psyche.

The simplest objection to Dr Guirdham's records is that he uses an alias to conceal the identity of all the patients who have benefited from psychic healing. But he argues that medical ethics prevent him from doing otherwise. If, like several of the people he describes, they are doctors, or patients who have specifically asked him not to reveal their identity, he can hardly break his word.

He defines two main kinds of psychic healing and backs up each definition with an array of personal case histories. In one kind of psychic healing the healer takes on the patient's symptoms. The second kind involves 'out of the body experiences' in which the healer appears to a patient who may be a vast distance away.

The principal difference between psychic healing and faith healing or laying-on-of-hands healing is that the psychic healer works involuntarily. Dr Guirdham stresses that while thousands of people can claim to heal by 'faith' or laying on hands, only very few, as far as he knows, have the ability to heal through their psyche.

Dr Guirdham cites his Miss Mills as the best example he knows of a psychic healer who works by assuming a sick person's symptoms. On one occasion the doctor and his wife had arranged to meet a woman doctor called Marion for lunch at Miss Mills's home. Marion phoned Dr Guirdham from 60 miles away some time before she was due to arrive to say that she had had a motor accident. She asked him to tell Miss Mills that she would come on to her house as soon as she could. She did not say that she had been hurt; but a little later she phoned again to say that she felt too bad to continue her journey.

Soon after receiving Marion's first call, Dr Guirdham was

surprised to get a call from Miss Mills asking, 'What has happened to Marion?' Miss Mills had had a premonition that Marion had been involved in some kind of accident, though she had had no direct message from her.

Later that afternoon after lunch Miss Mills – quite out of the blue – began to give a running commentary of what was happening to Marion. She told them that Marion had broken her leg, taken a taxi back to London, had been admitted to the casualty department of a teaching hospital. Her fracture had been confirmed by X-ray, and her leg had been put in plaster. (During this time no telephone call had come from Marion herself.)

Then, later in the afternoon, Miss Mills developed a limp. Examining her, Dr Guirdham found that the lower end of her right leg appeared to be badly bruised and very tender. As she had been under his eye all the time, he knew that she had not fallen down or suffered any injury which could have caused painful symptoms.

Later on that day Marion did phone again from London. Her account of what had happened coincided in every detail with Miss Mills's revelation. She confirmed that Miss Mills had related each incident at the same time as it was happening to her. She had suffered a Pott's fracture on her right leg, and the area of swelling and bruising coincided with Miss Mills's unexplained symptoms.

She also told them that, except for a few minutes immediately after her accident, she had felt no pain whatsoever, even when her bones were being set before being put into plaster. The pain had stopped, they realized, at the very same moment that Miss Mills had called the Guirdhams to ask what had happened to Marion. Marion went on to enjoy a quick and unusually pain-free recovery, while Miss Mills continued to feel pain from an injury she had not had.

On another occasion Miss Mills had bumped into Guirdham, apparently quite by chance, while he was taking an afternoon stroll. Suddenly in the course of conversation she announced that a mutual friend called Paul, an orthopaedic surgeon in the United States, had just been in a car crash. No sooner had she said this than her eyes became inflamed. Her eyelids went into spasm and closed almost completely.

Later that day Paul's wife telephoned from the USA to say that Paul had indeed been hurt in an accident. A truck had slewed across the road in front of his car; his windscreen had been shattered and fragments of glass had gone into his eyes. He had been seen by an ophthalmic surgeon and a plastic surgeon, who had told him that he would be scarred and his sight would be permanently affected. He had had 27 stithces in his face.

Strangely, Paul's wife, Annette, was not particularly perturbed. She said that her husband was not in pain, and that she knew that 'Auntie' (her name for Miss Mills) was 'looking after him'. Miss Mills's eyes remained inflamed for several days. Paul, however, suffered no impairment to his vision, had no scars, despite the 27 stitches, and remained quite free of pain.

Unlike some doctors who believe in strange, wonderful and inexplicable phenomena, Dr Guirdham has never felt any need to conceal his beliefs and experiences from his colleagues. Indeed he has been invited to lecture to fellow members of the Royal College of Psychiatrists, and even if he has not converted them wholesale to psychic healing, he has never been howled down as a fraud nor even encountered hostility. He is, as I described earlier, a highly credible person, orthodox, pragmatic and down to earth in inverse proportion to the other-worldliness of the experiences he describes. Another reason which has doubtless helped his credibility among colleagues is that many of the cases he describes involve other doctors.

In March 1974, Dr Charles, a psychiatrist who was a senior consultant at a famous Canadian hospital, contacted Dr Guirdham by phone to cancel a rendezvous he had arranged while he was on a course in England. He was suffering from a severe bout of 'flu, a cough and laryngitis, and his voice had been reduced to a squeak. Two days later the doctor with whom he was staying diagnosed pneumonia and a collapsed lung.

The next day Dr Guirdham had another call from Dr Charles to say that his pneumonia had vanished, his lung re-inflated, and that the only thing still troubling him was the squeaky voice. This sudden remission was amazing and could not be attributed to the antibiotics which he had been taking for only twelve hours prior to recovery.

The real reason Charles was calling was not so much to mention his recovery as the means by which it had been brought about. The previous night while he was lying ill in bed, a woman with luminous blue eyes, wearing a dark blue robe with a silver girdle and large cross on her chest, had materialized before him. 'She placed one hand above the site of my pneumonia and the other round the base of my thumb.' He felt a deep heat and tingling sensation on the points where she touched him.

Dr Guirdham recognized the manner in which she had laid hands on Charles as a healing technique favoured by the thirteenth-century Cathars. From Charles's description he also recognized the woman as the Braïda who was so familiar to Miss Mills. Charles went back to Canada with his voice as high pitched as ever. This symptom, which had originally been attributed to his upper respiratory tract infection, persisted. It was later diagnosed by a throat surgeon as a cancer of the larynx. Charles kept in regular contact with Dr Guirdham and said that the same woman was continuing to appear before him. She laid her hands on his throat and the back of his neck, and he experienced a similar sensation of deep, penetrating heat.

Meanwhile his surgeon had advised radiotherapy. But before treatment was due to begin, a second biopsy was made of the cancerous area to see whether the condition had grown worse. The pathologist was surprised to find that the tumour had in fact grown smaller. Treatment was postponed for a few days. Dr Charles continued to feel the woman in blue's hands on his throat and neck, and at the next examination it was found that the cancer had completely disappeared.

Not content to let an apparent miracle rest, Dr Charles described his case to a meeting of his hospital clinical society and asked whether any of his colleagues could come up with a reasonable explanation. The pathologist told the meeting that the condition could not have been wrongly diagnosed and offered to display the biopsy tissue samples to anyone who doubted it. Spontaneous remission, a phenomenon which does occur from time to time with cancer, was ruled out because when it does happen it does not occur so rapidly.

Braïda has appeared on the other side of the Atlantic several times. In the autumn of 1975 the teenage son of another Canadian psychiatrist, a friend of Dr Charles, caught viral meningitis. Within 24 hours he was dangerously ill and delirious with a temperature of 105°F, a terrible headache and extreme pain in his neck.

Suddenly and inexplicably the boy's fever abated. Despite the original severity of his symptoms, he returned to almost normal health in the space of half a day. As soon as his delirium had gone and his temperature fallen, he asked his father to explain 'who was the woman in the dark blue robe with the blue eyes' who had appeared and put one hand on his forehead and another on his wrist. The boy said that the mysterious lady had given him a feeling of great peace and had banished his headache with a touch of her hand.

Dr Guirdham has himself practised psychic healing – albeit unwittingly – and benefited from it during illness. He not infrequently receives telephone calls from grateful patients or their relatives, thanking him for appearing at their bedside many miles or continents away dressed in his own Cathar robes. These excursions often occur when he is asleep and he knows nothing about them until he is told by the patients.

Once, while on holiday in the Isle of Wight, he hurt himself badly in a fall. He felt a sharp pain in the sixth, seventh and eighth ribs and concluded that he had either cracked the bones or severely bruised them. He did not see a doctor, firstly because he did not want to cut into his holiday, and secondly because there was little good a doctor could have done anyway. In those days a doctor would have strapped up his chest; nowadays the fashion is to leave it unstrapped. Either way prompt medical treatment did not appear to offer any immediate practical advantage. This is how he described the ensuing sequence of events:

> Because my pain intensified towards evening and moving of the arm was becoming more painful, I addressed a sudden, unspoken distress message to a friend with an unequalled healing capacity living 80 miles from the island. I felt the contact of hands on my ribs and arm and the same sensation of deep penetrating heat described by Dr Charles.
>
> Next morning I felt remarkably better. My ribs were far less painful and I could move my arm freely. I received a telephone call from a woman in Switzerland, herself psychic, who asked how I was. The previous day she had been certain I had had an accident. She had phoned my friend, with whom I had made no contact in the material senses of the word, and had been told the exact time of the accident. This awareness of disaster, by means of somatic telepathy, exhibited by individuals living on the same wavelength but living at a distance, is a frequent accompaniment of psychic healing.

While being 'on the same wavelength' is clearly a very significant feature of psychic healing, Dr Guirdham stresses that it is not some kind of informal service operated between friends. Even though he did subsequently become close to the individuals who had shared his Cathar incarnation, they had not previously been friends in this life. They had met *apparently* by chance. Psychic healing is performed unconsciously; the healer's psyche moves quite independently of the healer's conscious mind and body, and appears to obey no rules but its own. The one thing which facilitates psychic healing is having known the 'patients' in previous lives.

Indeed the psyche and the personality are often seen to be at odds. Like the American Dr Ian Stevenson, whose own views of reincarnation will be discussed later, Dr Guirdham's work as a child psychiatrist has convinced him that personality disorders, especially obsessional conditions, are hangovers from previous incarnations, and that the disorder is caused by a rebellious psyche which is ill-adapted to the mould of the child's personality. He has observed that disturbed children are often the product of difficult labour or have been delivered by Caesarian section. 'Women who have to undergo Caesarian often turn out to be psychic,' he told me. 'They do want the child, but something in their unconscious tells them not to incarnate another spirit.'

There are of course much more straightforward anatomical reasons why women have to undergo Caesarian section. Dr Guirdham does not try to deny this but points out that a difficult labour is not invariably attributable to a narrow birth passage.

The problem which faces any uncommitted commentator on Dr Guirdham's claims is that the good doctor offers a great deal of experience but no evidence. He conceals the identity of his Cathar companions and their patients, justifying this with perfectly reasonable recourse to conventional medical ethics. And, of course, even if one could manage to track them down to tell their own account of the events, one would still have no irrefutable proof that these things took place, even assuming that they did.

The series of coincidences which brought his female Cathar companions to him in this life might seem too good to be true. But if one can accept the idea that nothing in this world happens by chance, and that our lives are part of a divinely inspired pattern, a cosmic kaleidoscope in which little glass beads are being constantly reshuffled to form fresh designs, then such coincidences are quite acceptable. This is a holistic approach echoed in the beliefs of most of the people whose work is described in this book.

You might decide that the whole business is a fabrication, dreamed up by an ingenious old gentleman with an unusual sense of humour. In the final analysis I am sure you will believe what you like.

10 Psychic Surgery—Corncobs and Country Bumpkins

Spiritualism and spiritism have been widely regarded as refuges for weak-minded people who refuse to come to terms with what everybody else believes to be reality.

The West (by which I mean those people who adhere to the cultural values of Europe and North America) is alone in its rejection of such phenomena, however. Possession by discarnate spirits is accepted as fact in Africa, South America, the Philippines, the Far East and indeed by the Eskimoes too. People who are patently not weak-minded are as confirmed in their belief as Westerners are in their disbelief.

There may be small differences in ritual between nations where psychic healing is practised, but the philosophy is essentially similar. The main principles are that some, if not all, disease is caused by the invasion of spirits, and, more important, that the psychic healer is only the agent of psychic forces who use him as a tool.

A significant moving force in the development of psychic healing over the past 150 years was the French spiritualist Alain Kardec who, for a short period at least, attracted many nineteenth-century French intellectuals and professionals to his theory that healing could be effected through mediums. Kardec's main influence, however, has been in Brazil and the Philippines, both polyglot nations with a heady blend of diverse cultures.

In Brazil Kardec's spiritist philosophy is upheld by sects made up of undeniably educated people from the country's professional elite. Indeed, there are two Kardecist hospitals where doctors use mediums as an adjunct to conventional medicine. There are also the Umbanda and Quimbanda movements, which are less acceptable to intellectuals but which are inspired directly by the religious and medical traditions imported by Yoruba African slaves two hundred years ago.

In the Philippines the city of Manila has lately established its reputation as the Lourdes of the Pacific. The country has hundreds of practitioners who claim to perform, and in some cases do perform, remarkable surgical feats at a distance or with their bare hands.

Unfortunately, many of these psychic surgeons have been shown to be charlatan conjurors as far as their surgical techniques are concerned. In 1975 a British TV film team revealed that the blood, tissue and tumours which healers claimed to have excised from their patients turned out to be taken from chickens or pigs.

Although many of the patients said at the time that their symptoms had gone, follow-up visits showed that their cure had been illusory and had dissipated shortly after leaving the emotionally charged environment of the healer's clinic.

David Hoy, an experienced investigator of psychic phenomena who has great experience in spotting fraudulent practice, witnessed five Philippino healers at work and reported that all used classic conjuring techniques. (*Healers and the Healing Process*, ed. George Meek, Quest Books, 1978.)

The biologist and anthropologist Dr Lyall Watson has done his own study of Philippino healers and come to a different conclusion. He admits that much of the blood, viscera and other bits and pieces which the healer claims to remove from patients do on analysis turn out to be animal tissues. He is adamant, however, that these objects are not palmed by the healer as a conjuror might palm a playing card, but actually materialize while the healer is at work. He reports that pieces of marked cotton wool have been put into a patient's ear six inches in front of his doubting eyes and withdrawn by the healer from the patient's other ear. One healer, Juan Blance, who specializes in treating eye complaints, touches the patient's eyelid, and out pops 'a bean-shaped, green doughy mess . . . which seems to bring immediate remission of the problem'. Another healer, Jose Mercado, goes in for 'spirit injections'. He lines his patients up and passes them at a distance of about six feet, pointing his finger at their arms and exclaiming 'Zip, zip, zip'. Dr Watson put this technique to the test by wrapping a sheet of plastic round his arm under his shirt and joining the line of patients. After being zipped he found that his arm had been pricked and had bled slightly and that a pinprick hole had appeared in the plastic sheet.

Juan Blance was able to make a shallow incision in the skin of Watson's chest by simply pointing his finger at the body a foot away from the chest itself. Watson was covered by a plastic sheet on this occasion too, but this time the cut appeared in his skin without any damage being done to the plastic. Another healer, Josephine Sison, specializes in removing foreign objects from her patients' bodies. These are not the kind of objects one might expect to have caused the patient's illness: they include things like 'an entire corncob, ten inches long, complete with fruit, a plastic bag, a six-inch rusty nail, or a piece of glass'.

Several scientists who watched Josephine Sison working at very close range, are convinced that the techniques did not depend on sleight of hand, and that the objects or incisions – in Watson's words – 'materialized at the interface between healer and patient. They are there from one moment to the next, between one frame of the film and the next. The method is very effective, perhaps because some tangible object is apparently removed.'

The most famous Philippino healer is Tony Agpaoa. Unlike most Philippino healers, who appear to be in a trance-like state while doing their work, Agpaoa looks conscious and alert when he operates. He performed scores of operations in the presence of scientists and doctors from the USA and West Germany, and underwent laboratory investigation by the psychologist Professor Hiroshi Motoyama in Tokyo.

In all of these operations Agpaoa withdrew diseased tissue or parts of organ from the patient after using nothing but his bare hands to 'open' the body. Sometimes he would use a pair of unsterilized scissors to snip off the tissue he wanted to remove. He wore a short sleeved shirt – so he could not have concealed anything up his sleeve – and the whole process was filmed.

The word 'open' above needed inverted commas, because both the film and eye witness accounts showed that he did not actually penetrate the flesh. His hands would press on the area above the site of the disease, and tumours and blood would emerge from between his fingers.

In his book *Healers and the Healing Process*, George Meek points out that Philippino healers began to introduce blood and tissue into their operations only when Western foreigners came seeking treatment. Whereas their native patients were brought up on the idea of disease being caused by 'witchcraft items' such as a corncob or nail, Westerners associated surgery with blood and guts – and that is what they got!

Bizarre problems have also beset film crews and others. When Lyall Watson was working with a German crew the film makers wanted to get convincing evidence that a healer could in fact make an incision by paranormal methods. For this purpose they found a patient with an artificial metal hip joint and a healer who was prepared to demonstrate his skills by operating on the leg. Their idea was that if they could photograph the exposed metal, this would offer convincing evidence that a real incision had been made. In the event what happened was that as soon as the healer opened the hip, the camera lights failed – something which had not happened in three weeks of filming.

Many psychics have been reported to have the ability consciously, but more often unconsciously to jam machinery, affect photographic film and interfere with magnetic tape recordings, as well as to make objects materialize and disappear. In one incident an Italian surgeon whose patient had had a gallstone removed by Tony Agpaoa, sealed the stone in a bottle and took it back with him on the plane to match it against X-ray photographs he had taken in Italy. When he got back home he found that the specimen bottle, which was still sealed, no longer contained the stone.

Such things do not aid investigation; they just make the converted even more convinced that paranormal powers are at work, and make sceptics more sceptical.

Less controversial and more amazing than the Philippino psychic surgeons was the Brazilian healer Jose Pedro de Freitas, universally known by his nickname Arigo. I say Arigo was less controversial because his operations were witnessed by scores of doctors and scientists, nearly all of whom were highly sceptical of his activities before seeing him at work, but who were subsequently forced to admit that he was performing miracles. Arigo – the name means 'bumpkin' – was put on trial twice by the Brazilian authorities, once for practising medicine illegally and once for practising witchcraft. Not one witness could be found to prove that his skills were fraudulent; indeed the success of the prosecutions was due entirely to the evidence of cured patients who vouched that he had treated them successfully!

An excellent biography of the man (he died in 1971) and an account of the scientific studies made of his work has been made by the American journalist John G. Fuller in his book *Arigo – Surgeon of the Rusty Knife*. Briefly, the story runs thus:

Arigo was a short, powerfully built miner living in the small Brazilian town of Congonhas do Campo. He was a popular extrovert, whose attempts to unionize his fellow workers and organize a strike had led to him being fired from his job. He then ran a bar in Congonhas. He was a devout, practising Catholic, married and with several children.

In the late 1940s, when Arigo was thirty years old, he began to be troubled by strange dreams in which he was addressed by a gruff German voice. The dreams which often made him wake up with a headache became increasingly vivid, until one night they assumed the proportions of hallucination. Arigo found himself watching a surgical operation being conducted by a fat, bossy, bald German doctor. This doctor proceeded to tell Arigo that he was Dr Adolpho Fritz, who had practised in

Eastern Europe and had died during the First World War. Arigo was told that he had been chosen to carry on the doctor's work, and that the spirit of Dr Fritz and other deceased medical men would act through him to cure the sick. Arigo awoke from this dream in terror and rushed screaming down the village street.

Spiritism and the influence of the Kardec sect were resented by the Church in Brazil and when Arigo confided his dream to the village priest, he was urged to pay no heed to these devilish dream voices. The dreams persisted, however, and the more Arigo tried to fight off Dr Fritz, the more he became afflicted with blinding headaches.

Arigo's ability to resist Dr Fritz's call collapsed spectacularly. One night in 1950 in the Hotel Financial in the city of Belo Horizonte, Arigo was staying in the same hotel as Senator Lucio Bittencourt, a Brazilian politician who had brought Arigo and some friends to the city for a political rally. Some weeks previously Bittencourt had been told by his doctor that he had a lung cancer and needed immediate surgery. Bittencourt had told nobody about this, and as he was in the middle of a political campaign, he had put off acting on his doctor's advice.

Very late that evening he was lying in bed trying to sleep when Arigo entered the room with glazed eyes – with a razor blade in his hand. He walked over to the Senator, who felt strangely unable to resist, and proceeded to cut him open, muttering in the thick German accent as he did so. Bittencourt blacked out but was able to recall the incident the next morning. There was blood on his pyjamas and an almost healed incision over his ribs. When he told Arigo what had happened, the bewildered peasant was at a loss to explain and said he remembered nothing. When Bittencourt subsequently visited his doctor, he said nothing about the midnight apparition until the doctor had X-rayed him, congratulated him for taking his advice, and declared that the tumour had gone.

Shortly afterwards Arigo, having returned to his home town, was called with his wife and friends to the house of a neighbour who was dying from a cancer of the womb. She had been given the Last Rites and the people had gathered to pay their last respects. Suddenly Arigo was taken over by the persona of Dr Fritz. He rushed out to the kitchen, returned with a bread knife, and before the astonished gaze of the neighbours, plunged the instrument up the woman's vagina. Having made a few brisk movements with the knife, he reached inside the body and pulled out a large tumour, which was identified by the woman's doctor as a uterine cancer. The woman recovered her health.

Within a few months 300 patients were queuing outside Arigo's house every day, and it has been estimated by Fuller that in the following five years he treated and cured half a million people, including the daughter of the Brazilian president who had been suffering from leukaemia. Arigo's operations were witnessed by so many people, including scores of doctors from Brazil and the USA, that little doubt can be attached to his miraculous skill and his complete lack of chicanery.

Patients who did not need surgery were given bizarre prescriptions which Arigo would write after merely glancing at them. The scrips would generally include an illogical mixture of drugs, some obsolete, some so new that they were barely known in the USA, let alone Brazil. The concoctions invariably worked, though when curious doctors tried to prescribe them to their own patients no benefit ensued.

Whenever he was working Arigo assumed the gruff, imperious German accent of Dr Fritz, and he even replied in German when asked questions in that language which he had never learnt. He never made any attempt at antisepsis and used kitchen knifes, penknives, scissors or indeed any useful blade which came to hand. And even though his surgical movements were crude his patients never flinched or felt pain. Films have been made of Arigo cutting tissue out of patients' eyes with scissors while the patient stands still and calm.

No one has the least idea how he did it, of course. Dr Andrija Puharich the American doctor who later became famous – nay, notorious – for his studies of Uri Geller, found that a 'repulsive force' – like the energy you feel when you try to hold the like poles of two magnets together – seemed to act between Arigo's instrument and the flesh he was cutting.

Puharich himself felt this force on the occasion when Arigo grabbed his hand and told him to stick a penknife in a patient's eye. Under Arigo's guidance Puharich was able to move the knife freely in the eye socket without causing any damage.

This repulsive force could not be explained in conventional electromagnetic terms, however. Puharich carried out all the regular bioelectrical measurements on Arigo while he was operating, but he found no abnormal reading which could account for this mysterious repulsion between metal and tissue.

Arigo is not unique in Brazil. Many other healers have been studied, and most act, like Arigo, under the control of 'a spirit'. Why Brazil should be so replete with psychic surgeons is difficult to explain. Certainly the country's cultural and religious history fosters belief in reincarnation and spiritism, and this may explain why Brazilians are more prepared to offer themselves for psychic surgery than, say, Anglo-Saxons. But it does not explain how an untutored man with a pair of dirty scissors can cut out a cancer without infecting the patient or causing pain.

11 Reincarnation—Come Again

In a mushroom-coloured wooden frame house, tucked away
in the trees behind Howard Johnson's motel in Charlottesville,
Virginia, Dr Ian Stevenson has pondered the case histories of
1600 children from all over the world. To most European and
American psychiatrists the tales told by these children would
suggest a diagnosis of schizophrenia, to most teachers an
incorrigible addiction to falsehood, and to most parents a
social embarrassment which they would do their best to hide
from the neighbours. For Dr Stevenson they offer strong
evidence for a theory of reincarnation.

For the average Western parent it would be quite unnerving
if their infant child were to announce that it has lived this life
before as another person and then proceed to recite in-
numerable facts and demonstrate remarkable adult skills to
prove the point.

In the Far East parents might be happy to accept the idea
that their child's body housed the personality of some departed
individual, but in the West the notion of reincarnation is an
affront to every dearly-held belief. Christians believe in resur-
rection but eschew the idea of soul transmigration. Materialists
assume that mind and personality are functions of the brain and
must surely disappear when the brain decays. And Western
parents, schooled in the precepts of biology, believe that they
make their babies. Steeped in proprietorial pride, the last
thing they want to hear is that baby has become the receptacle
of some drifting spirit from the realms of the dead.

Even among parapsychologists (the people who used to be
called psychic researchers) reincarnation is widely thought to
be a disreputable subject. Professor J. B. Rhine, of Duke
University, North Carolina, the first serious academic to

secure parapsychology a footing in a university department, discouraged Ian Stevenson from pursuing the subject.

'Like many others, he could see no sense in it,' Dr Stevenson recalls. 'He thought that a line had to be drawn somewhere, and he drew the line at reincarnation.'

The problem for Stevenson, however, was that he was faced with a lot of facts which could not simply be dismissed by having a dogmatic line drawn through them. As an academic psychiatrist he had begun collecting accounts of people who claimed that they remembered previous lives. Within a few years he had built up a dossier of scores of reports which he had collected during his spare time and university vacations. By 1957 Stevenson was head of the department of psychiatry at the University of Virginia Medical School and subsequently published two well-received books on conventional psychiatry. His reputation had been founded on his shrewd, thoroughgoing, scientific approach to his speciality. Yet despite his high position in the academic establishment, he found himself being drawn increasingly towards a subject which even the most way out researchers regard as 'unscientific'.

The reason why otherwise sympathetic scientists had steered well clear of reincarnation is that the mass of evidence was anecdotal, uncheckable and came from dubious sources. As often as not, stories which show the most compelling *prima facie* evidence of an individual remembering details of a previous life yield to quite simple explanation.

In *A Scientific Report on 'The Search for Bridey Murphy,'* the classic study on reincarnation, Dr Harold Rosen mentions a young man who, under hypnosis, uttered curses in a strange language which was eventually identified as Oscan, an ancient Italian dialect spoken around the third century BC. Subsequent investigation by the hypnotist revealed that, some weeks earlier, the young man had been daydreaming in a library and his eyes had alighted on a textbook taken out by another student which described this ancient tongue. He had unconsciously taken in a number of phrases which were only brought out again when he was in a hypnotic trance. In his

179

waking state he denied having any idea where these ancient curses came from.

Dr Stevenson cites the warning example of an English army officer and his wife who, travelling in a part of the country neither had previously visited, came across a wayside pool which they both simultaneously 'recognized'. So baffled were they by this that they came to the hasty conclusion that they had lived together near this pool in some former life. It was only when they returned to London and revisited an art gallery where they had dropped in before their holiday that they saw the same wayside pool in a picture which they had quite forgotten setting eyes on.

There are currently at least three British hypnotists, and certainly many more in the United States, who encourage their patients to undergo 'life regressions', during which they supposedly remember two, three or more lives during the space of a hypnotized half hour. The American clairvoyant Edgar Cayce also claimed the ability to 'read' his clients' previous lives.

The hypnotists' skills make for the most riveting radio shows, and Edgar Cayce's readings may have worked all kinds of psychotherapeutic benefits, but it is almost invariably impossible to verify these 'lives' beyond reasonable doubt. It is far from easy to ascertain whether a Roman centurion, Levantine sailor or medieval East Anglian bone-setter ever existed except in the mind of a hypnotized twentieth-century citizen. The American psychologist E. S. Zolik reported in the *Journal of Clinical Psychology* in 1958 how he had got hypnotized subjects to 'recall' highly plausible previous existences. Out of their trance they denied all knowledge of the personalities they had evoked during hypnosis. When they were hypnotized again and instructed to search their memory for the source of various pieces of information they had come up with during their life regressions, they were found to have concocted these memories of previous lives from long lost recollections of books they had read, plays they had seen and other snippets of experience.

Dr Norman Shealy, the American neurosurgeon, whose

work with various psychics is described in another chapter, regards life regression as a highly efficient form of psychotherapy, though he is not inclined to believe that it offers any evidence of reincarnation. He practises the technique himself on many of his patients suffering from psychological problems caused by chronic intractable pain, and told me of one case where it had given him and his patient a fresh insight. The patient was a young woman who had become paraplegic as the result of a gunshot wound. She had woken up in hospital after the event and her husband had told her that she had accidentally shot herself while handling the gun. She could not remember anything about the incident, and when she arrived at Shealy's clinic some years later she was still suffering from amnesia of the ten minutes prior to the accident. When Shealy hypnotized her into a life regression, she came out with an account of the life of Ann Boleyn. As is often the case in life regression, she did not give herself a surname, but she said her name was Ann and gave a good first-person description of the life of Henry the Eighth's second wife right up to the moment of her execution.

When she was brought round she said she remembered nothing of the 'life' she had related and could not imagine what it signified. But it had given Shealy a clue.

'You think your husband shot you, don't you?' he told her. She burst into tears and admitted that she had suspected that very thing ever since coming round in hospital. The last thing she could remember about the incident was having a flaming row with her husband. All the rest had been blotted out by the shock.

It is often said by literary wishful thinkers that 'everybody has a book inside them'. Should this be the case, and if we assume that any good book will contain up to twenty different characters, we might surmise that everybody has a score of reincarnations inside them too. The great difference between Dr Stevenson and the life regressionists, however, is that Stevenson has concentrated his studies on children aged between two and six years.

An infant just cannot have had the same exposure to fables,

stories, films, plays or other people as an adult, and is much less likely to have been deeply impregnated with religious notions of reincarnation which might prompt an adult to construct previous lives for himself. It was for this reason that Dr Stevenson decided to concentrate his attention on the accounts of very young children who claimed that they had lived before. By 1960 he had assembled scores of such accounts, and he selected 44 of the best documented cases for a paper which he published in the *Journal of the American Society for Psychical Research*.

The case of Shanta Devi, a little Indian girl from Dehli, gives the flavour of that paper. Shanta Devi had been born in 1926, and from the age of three, not long after she had learnt to speak, she began to announce to her bemused parents details about a life she had lived before in the town of Muttra, some 80 miles away from Delhi. She told her family that her name had been Lugdi, that she had been born in 1902, had belonged to the Choban caste and had been married to a cloth merchant called Kedar Nath Chaubey. She had died shortly after giving birth to a son.

Shanta Devi did not desist from making these announcements, and by the time she was nine years old her family resolved to settle the matter. They wrote to Kedar Nath Chaubey at the address Shanta Devi had given them in Muttra. During her life Shanta had never left Delhi, let alone visited Muttra, so it came as another surprise for her parents when Kedar Nath Chaubey himself replied to the letter and confirmed everything the little girl had recited to her parents. He then sent a relative of his to the girl's home and shortly afterwards made a personal visit without giving Shanta Devi or her family prior warning. Shanta Devi immediately identified the cloth merchant and his relative. Keen to put their daughter's remarkable claims to more serious scrutiny, her parents agreed to have her abilities tested by a committee of impartial observers belonging to neither her present nor her 'former' family. It was duly arranged that she should make a trip to Muttra. On arrival at the railway station in Muttra she identified another relative of Kedar Nath Chaubey in the middle of a large crowd of people. She was then put in a carriage whose driver was instructed to go wherever she directed. Before long she had guided the driver to Chaubey's house, which she recognized even though it had been painted a different colour since Lugdi's death. Outside the house she spotted an old Brahmin whom she correctly identified as Chaubey's father, and when she went into the house she was immediately able to tell her observers the location of particular rooms, cupboards and stores.

She then had herself taken to Lugdi's family home, where she picked out her former parents from a crowd of 50 people gathered in the house. In another house, that of Kedar Nath Chaubey's parents, she told her delighted witnesses that she had buried some money in the corner of one of the rooms. When a hole was dug on the spot nothing was found. In the face of her repeated insistence that she had left money buried in that spot, Kedar Nath Chaubey came forward and shame-facedly admitted that he had found and removed the money after Lugdi's death.

Throughout the investigation the ten-year-old girl had spoken to her former family in the local Muttra dialect and had used idioms and slang which had been popular before her visit and which had passed out of current usage.

The case of Shanta Devi was just one of many Dr Stevenson had collected by 1960, and he had begun to classify them according to the hard evidence each presented. The largest category, which comprised several hundred cases, included those which were of very little use to a scientist. Either there was no definite proof that the deceased person described by his supposed living reincarnation had ever existed, or the deceased person was such a well-known historic character that knowledge about his or her life could easily have been learnt by quite normal methods. There were also hundreds of published accounts of *déjà vu* experiences in which the author claimed to have had 'a feeling' that he had been at a certain spot 'at some other time'.

Into his second category Dr Stevenson classified 27 published cases of individuals who were able to give accurate details about places or events which they seemed not to have learnt by any normal method. Into the third category – the one which interested him most – he brought his 44 cases of individuals who could recall details of people, places and events in the lives of others who had died before they were born. These cases differed widely in the hardness of their evidence. In eleven cases the person who claimed to have lived before was able to produce less than six verifiable items of information about the previous existence. In another five cases the deceased and the living individuals belonged to the same family or families of close neighbours, so there was still a possibility that even a very young child could have constructed the previous life from snippets of information heard at home. The most solid category included some 28 cases, like that of Shanta Devi, in which the deceased and living individuals were unrelated, living in different towns or countries, and in which the child had been able to produce more than six verifiable facts about the life of the person as whom they claimed to have lived before.

Reincarnation is of course not the only possible explanation for Shanta Devi's remarkable talent, and when he presented his paper Dr Stevenson took pains to consider other means, both normal and paranormal, by which the children could have discovered information about their alleged previous lives.

The first and obvious alternative explanation is fraud. Although fraud could not be absolutely ruled out in the cases he had studied, it seemed an unlikely explanation, given that the children were so young and that in almost every case a host of relatives and observers would have had to be involved in the conspiracy. It could also be argued that in a country like India where most people believe in reincarnation, stories like Shanta Devi's would be readily accepted by gullible folk only too keen to have 'evidence' for their traditional beliefs. In fact, although 23 of those 44 cases came from India or Burma where reincarnation is widely accepted, thirteen came from Europe, and four came from the United States and Canada, where very few people believe in reincarnation. Moreover, even though Hindus and Buddhists do accept reincarnation, many consider that children who recall past lives are destined to die young. In some of the cases studied by Dr Stevenson, the children's parents had tried to stop their children talking about their previous lives and opposed attempts to verify the children's claims.

Another feasible explanation could be that the children – like Dr Rosen's hypnotized young man and the English army officer and his wife – had learnt their 'memories' from early experiences or bits of conversation they had picked up from their parents and had subsequently forgotten where the information came from. If this were the case, the children's parents would have to have forgotten implanting these memories in their children too. Even then Stevenson was left with 20 cases in which the parents had neither known the individual involved, nor the family to which he or she belonged, nor even the town or country in which the former personality had lived.

A further alternative explanation could have been provided by stretching the popular theory of the psychiatrist Jung, who suggested that everyone possesses a 'collective unconscious'. According to Jung's theory memories and modes of behaviour are passed from one generation to the next, and no matter what individual experiences a person has undergone during his life, certain symbols and concepts will exert a powerful influence on him and everyone else who belongs to the same culture. The way in which skills – like an aptitude for music or carpentry – and even instinctual behaviour – like a mother's care for her offspring – pass on from one generation to the next is still hardly understood. But of course in most of these cases under consideration there was no genetic link between the child and its previous personality. And while Jung postulated that 'race memories' could persist through the generations, these memories were general rather than particular and certainly bore no resemblance to the ability to remember people's names or to recall what colour so-and-so's house had been twenty years previously.

Having exhausted the more generally plausible explanations, Dr Stevenson then considered the possibility that the children had learnt about their previous lives through various forms of extra-sensory perception. Could they have read the minds of people who had known the deceased's personality? If they had been able to do this, it would seem reasonable that they should be able to use their telepathic powers to other ends too; but in fact only two of the 44 children had shown any evidence of paranormal abilities which did not relate to their memories of a previous life.

Plunging further into the *terrain vague* of parapsychology for explanations which would prove as strong as reincarnation, Dr Stevenson pondered on retrocognition, precognition, possession and the possibility that the children were in touch with discarnate entities who had departed this life and were communicating from beyond. All these phenomena have been reported and written up in parapsychological literature, but they did not seem to fit the children.

Retrocognition, for instance, in which the person recalls past events about which they could not have obtained knowledge by normal means, is usually achieved in a state of trance or meditation or is set off by the person concentrating on an object associated with the event. In precognition the seer is able to predict the outcome of future events. But of course Stevenson's children were not looking into the future but recalling the past.

Accounts of discarnate entities who communicate with the living tend to be as dubious as the life regressions I mentioned earlier. The sensitives who received such communications appear to mix a good deal of wild fantasy with the verifiable facts they obtain. Moreover, the mediums who do communicate with discarnate entities usually manage to contact several such spirits, unlike the children who could only remember one previous life.

The final possible alternative Stevenson considered – possession – also differed in various important respects. Possession is the term used to describe experiences in which a person's body appears to become totally controlled by some deceased and/or discarnate personality. Accounts of possession tend to come from two sources. They either happen to mediums at seances: the medium goes into a trance and assumes the voice, attitudes and other mannerisms of a dead person, usually one known to the observers. Alternatively, a living person, often a child, is apparently taken over by the personality of a dead person. The possession occurs quite involuntarily as far as the person on the receiving end is concerned, and can last for months or years, though it usually happens spasmodically and passes after a few minutes. One of the best documented cases is that of Lurancy Vennum, a young American girl, who at the end of the last century was seemingly possessed by Mary Roff, a local girl who had died when Lurancy was 15 months old. Lurancy's apparent possession lasted several months, during which time she assumed the personality of the dead girl and disclosed a great many more details of Mary's life than she could possibly have picked up by any normal fashion.

The difference between such cases of possession and Dr Stevenson's children was that none of the children had ever been taken over completely by the personality from their previous life. Although they might have revealed a surprising knowledge of a previous life and even expressed a preference for that life over the one they were currently being obliged to live, they never claimed that their bodies were under the control of a discarnate entity.

While he found it impossible to deny that some of his cases could be explained by one or more of the hypotheses just outlined, Dr Stevenson had found all these explanations wanting to a greater or lesser degree. As he saw it, the notion which explained them most satisfactorily was reincarnation, the idea that personality could pass from a dead person to a newborn child. He did not suggest that he had proof of reincarnation, but concluded:

The evidence I have assembled and reviewed does not warrant any firm conclusion about reincarnation. But it does

187

justify, I believe, a much more extensive and more sympathetic study of this hypothesis than it has hitherto received in the West.

Western civilization, let alone Western psychiatry, was not yet ready to clasp reincarnation to its bosom, however. Dr Stevenson's paper had appeared in the *Journal of the American Society for Psychical Research*, a publication which most scientists and lay people regard as 'fringe' to say the least. Moreover, his study had been based on case reports which he had not compiled and which went back 50 years or more. If he was to make his theory more plausible, he would have to find many more cases to investigate at first hand.

Some people did regard his work as extremely significant, however. The American Society for Psychical Research awarded him a prize, and Mrs Eileen Garrett, the famous medium, dug into her own pocket and gave him a grant to investigate what appeared to be a strong reincarnation case which had just been reported in India. It was largely through Mrs Garrett's generosity that he was able to pursue his studies during the next few years.

During the next 17 years Dr Stevenson travelled throughout the world, to India, Ceylon, Thailand, Japan, the Near East, Europe, South America, Alaska and within the United States. He investigated over a thousand cases, all children who had had similar experiences to Shanta Devi. His work was tolerated with a certain amount of amusement at the University of Virginia where he became regarded as a harmless eccentric. His reputation in conventional psychiatry discouraged most antagonistic sceptics from attacking him outright.

In the mid-1960s his silent critics began to get alarmed, however. Chester Carlson, the multi-millionaire inventor of the xerograph photocopying process, whose wife had had remarkable psychic abilities, decided to pour real money into parapsychological research. He offered to fund a new Division of Parapsychology at the University and encouraged Dr Stevenson to become its director and to bring in researchers from other universities who had been engaged in their own research into the paranormal.

'The critics who had been hiding behind the bushes suddenly realized that we were in earnest,' Dr Stevenson recalls. 'And they came out strongly with all the old criticisms of parapsychology – that it was unscientific, riddled with fraud, and could make a laughing stock of the University.'

Although he was able to set up the new Division of Parapsychology, he encountered more problems when Chester Carlson died and left a million dollars to the University on the condition that it be used exclusively for parapsychological research, and Stevenson's work on reincarnation in particular. There were great debates in the University as to whether the bequest should be accepted. 'Some people just wished that Chester Carlson's will and money would disappear. Fortunately though there is a strong tradition of freedom of enquiry at the University which they could not gainsay.'

'The University of Virginia was founded by President Jefferson, who not only opposed the 'political tyranny of the British but had declared himself an enemy of intellectual tyranny too. He had laid down that scholars should be able to pursue any idea as long as their work was left open to scrutiny and the possibility of refutation.'

Finally the bequest was accepted and the reincarnation project allowed to continue.

Sadly there is not enough space in a brief account to go into every detail of the evidence Dr Stevenson accumulated and the steps he took to ensure that he was not bamboozled by the witnesses. Unlike many scientific theories, reincarnation could not be tested in the laboratory. He had to adopt the research methods of the lawyer and historian, who can only seek after the truth by sifting through a mass of testimony from individual observers. He pursued every case by interviewing as many as twenty witnesses of the children's utterances. The validity of the child's and its parents' claims were checked by intensive questioning of the family to which the supposedly reincarnate person had belonged. He scrutinized medical records for facts about the dead person and interviewed independent witnesses connected with neither family.

In most cases he only arrived on the scene long after the child had started to announce the news of its previous life. But sometimes he was lucky enough to interview the child at the same time as it was recalling what it claimed to be its previous existence. He was then able to check the accuracy of those 'memories' at first hand.

A five-year-old Lebanese boy, Imad Elawar, offered one such opportunity. On a research trip to Brazil in 1963 Dr Stevenson had used the services of a Lebanese interpreter who had shown a great deal of interest in his work. The interpreter suggested that the doctor should visit the Lebanon because, he said, that country, and one section of its community in particular, had many children who recalled past lives.

The recent civil war in Lebanon has shown us how culturally and politically divided that country is. One group who found themselves in the middle of the war were the Druses, an Islamic sect who live a rural life in villages some distance from the big cities. It was these people whom the interpreter urged Stevenson to visit, and he gave him the name and address of his brother who lived in the village of Kornayel, where, he said, a number of supposed reincarnations had been reported over recent years.

Ian Stevenson does not speak Arabic, though he can speak French, the second language of the Lebanon. In March 1964, accompanied by an interpreter who could speak English, French and Arabic, he went to Kornayel. In the village he learnt that indeed a number of reincarnations had been reported over the years and that at that very moment there was a young boy in the village who had been making such claims.

The boy's name was Imad, the son of Mohammed Elawar. Imad had been born on 21 December 1958. When he was barely two years old he had begun to mention names which meant nothing to his parents. As, with the passing months, he learnt to speak properly and put sentences together, the names became part of statements and questions he put to his parents. He would ask them to tell him how Jamile, Fuad and Huda were getting on. He asked for news about various 'brothers' and 'friends' in the village of Khriby, a community some miles away which neither he nor – so they claimed – his parents had ever visited. He spoke these names in his sleep and at odd moments of the day. By the time of Dr Stevenson's arrival in Kornayel he had recited to his parents a bewildering mish-mash of facts about the life he had led in Khriby. He had said that his name was Bouhamzy, he had talked about his house and his love of hunting. He had mentioned on many occasions the female name Jamile and had said that Jamile wore red clothes and high-heeled shoes. Once, when he was just three and a half, he had lain on his mother's bed, embraced her and asked her to 'Do what Jamile does'. At other times he had said how much prettier Jamile was than his mother. He sub-sequently recalled with some vehemence a road accident in which a truck had driven over a man's legs. He would cry out that the truck driver had deliberately run the victim over and was a murderer. On another occasion he mentioned how pleased he was 'to be up and about'.

Imad's father told Stevenson that he had scolded the boy for telling these tales and had called him a liar. The result was that the boy stopped talking about Khriby and its inhabitants in front of his father but confided what he had to say about his previous life to his mother and grandparents, who lived in the same house.

One day a villager from Khriby had come over to Kornayel – a rare event – and had been recognized and identified by Imad. This suggested to the boy's parents that it might be a good idea to take his claims more seriously. When the next visitor from Khriby came to the village they asked her whether she was familiar with any of the names cited by Imad, and the woman confirmed that all were or had been inhabitants of the village.

By the time Dr Stevenson reached Kornayel Imad's parents were beginning to grow weary of their little boy's demands that they should take him to Khriby. They had not done so, however, and this offered Stevenson a chance to test the boy's abilities for himself. First he made a reconnoitre of Khriby.

There he learnt from villagers he questioned that there was indeed a family called Bouhamzy, and that a man called Said Bouhamzy had been run over by a truck several years earlier and had later died of his injuries. The only problem was, however, that someone else in the area had already claimed to be Said's reincarnation! Not only that, but Imad's description of his former home in Khriby bore little resemblance to Said Bouhamzy's residence.

These apparent contradictions had Stevenson stymied for a while, until he learnt that there were many Bouhamzys in Khriby. Said, he was told, had had a cousin Ibrahim, who died in 1949 aged 25. Ibrahim had been a forceful and popular personality in the village, a keen huntsman and had had a mistress – a very beautiful girl called Jamile. Since Ibrahim's death she had married and moved away. The cause of Ibrahim's death had been tuberculosis which had left him bed-ridden for the last months of his life. Ibrahim had been a great friend of Said, the doctor was told, and had been desolated to hear of his death. He had refused to believe that the truck driver had run Said over accidentally.

On 19 March 1964, Stevenson accompanied Mohammed Elawar and Imad on the boy's first trip to Khriby. First stop was Said Bouhamzy's house. Imad appeared very shy about entering the place and said that he recognized nothing there. Across the street in the house where Ibrahim had lived he reacted very differently.

In Ibrahim's house Imad identified a young woman, whose name had often cropped up before in his 'memories', as Huda, Ibrahim's sister. Taken aback more than somewhat by the boy's ability, someone showed Imad an oil painting of a young man dressed in traditional Arab costume.

'It's Fuad,' the boy exclaimed, clutching the picture to his chest. Again he was right. Fuad had been Ibrahim's younger brother, and the two had been very close. He was then shown another picture, but this time the Bouhamzys deliberately tried to trip him up.

'That's your brother Fuad too,' one of them told him.

'No, it's your uncle – don't you recognize him?' another suggested.

'You are wrong,' the boy protested. 'It's not them. It's me!'

It was indeed a portrait of Ibrahim.

En route to Khriby Imad had given Stevenson ten new facts about Ibrahim and about the village he had never visited. Checking these claims with the Bouhamzys, Stevenson found that the boy had been wrong in three of these assertions but that the rest had been quite accurate. Among the points the boy had made before visiting the Bouhamzy home – and which Stevenson subsequently verified – were that Ibrahim had owned a little yellow car; that he had had cherry and apple trees in his garden; and that he had had a dog which was kept attached to a cord in the yard. The cord was a particularly significant detail; dogs in the area were usually tethered by a chain, but, as it turned out, Ibrahim had bound his dog with a cord instead.

For the Bouhamzys the boy's most startling revelation was his recall of Ibrahim's dying words. Huda, who had been with Ibrahim when he died, asked Imad what his last words had been in his previous life.

'Huda, call Fuad!' the boy answered.

Huda assured Dr Stevenson that those had indeed been the man's last words. On the point of death he had wanted to see his older brother. In fact he died before his brother could be found.

In total Imad recalled over 70 facts about what he claimed to have been his previous life before and after Stevenson's arrival in Kornayel. Some of these had been 'remembered' in the doctor's presence, and the great majority of them were verified by Stevenson by checking and cross-checking with members of the Bouhamzy family and apparently disinterested villagers who had known the man.

Imad Elawar is just one of several hundred children investigated by Dr Stevenson which he describes as 'cases suggestive of reincarnation'. He does not rashly claim that they prove reincarnation, but rather that, taken as a body, reincarnation offers the most satisfactory explanation for them. Taken individually these cases can easily be faulted by a sceptic. How, for instance, can we be certain that the whole Imad Elawar case was not a put-up job, a deliberate fraud by the interpreter who suggested his visit to Lebanon, the Elawar family and the Bouhamzy family?

In his own writings Dr Stevenson has pointed out that investigation is no simple matter.

When he reaches the scene, much depends on the investigator's skill as an interviewer in eliciting and analysing the testimony.

The skill of the interviewer should never be casually assumed in such enquiries. Granting, however, a sufficient skill in the interviewer, a central difficulty of all such enquiries lies in the unreliability of the memories and even perceptions of the experience in the witnesses, who may omit or import various details of the case and thus alter it, sometimes immeasurably, from an accurate representation of actual events. Such alterations of memory may arise from deficiencies of intelligence in the reporting person, or from errors manufactured by his wishes or fears or in confronting something of emotional significance to him. But if we ask how we detect such errors in relation to the 'real events' in any enquiry, we have to acknowledge that we do this by comparing what one informant said with what some other informant said or wrote about the same event. We can never escape in science, even in the laboratory, from human testimony of some kind. The task is that of testing and improving, rather than discarding such testimony.

The evidence Dr Stevenson has collected over the past 20 years is of the kind which might be presented and accepted in a court of law. But evidence which would convince a judge and jury might not satisfy a scientist who likes to back his theories with double blind trials and repeatable laboratory experiments. Until recently Stevenson's reports on his continuing investigations were largely confined to the pages of the *Journal of the American Society for Psychical Research*. But in September 1977 he achieved a breakthrough. The editors of the *Journal of Nervous and Mental Disease*, a highly and widely respected medical journal, were persuaded that his theory of reincarnation was backed by such a weight of scrupulously researched material that it deserved wider consideration.

Dr Stevenson used that opportunity not only to outline the history of his own and other serious researchers' thoughts on the possibility of reincarnation but also to suggest how the reincarnation theory could explain an array of psychiatric disorders and health problems which were still poorly understood by conventional medicine.

Phobias

Phobias – irrational fears – not uncommonly affect young children. Sometimes they can be explained simply as the result of some traumatic, frightening event in early infancy. A child who has been bitten by a dog, for instance, might develop a fear of dogs which would manifest itself as a paralysing anxiety or a psychosomatic complaint such as asthma.

Often, however, no simple explanation can be found for an irrational fear. In the course of his research Dr Stevenson came across many children with phobias which could be traced back to their previous lives. Three children who had been delivered from their previous lives by drowning, for instance, had a phobia for water. A Lebanese boy who had previously died in a car crash was terrified of motor vehicles; an Alaskan boy who had been stabbed to death in his former life could not bear the sight of bladed weapons or tools; and an Indian child whose previous personality had come to mortal grief after catching food poisoning by eating a contaminated dish of curds would be terror struck at the prospect of that same dish. Several other children had phobias for particular places, which turned out to be the same spot on which they said they had met a violent end to their previous incarnation.

Philias

The opposite of a phobia is a philia, an abnormally strong

interest, attraction or appetite. Such predilictions were even more noticeable among the children than phobias and more often than not reflected strangely adult tastes in such young children. Three children Dr Stevenson studied expressed a great love of alcohol very early in life. In their previous incarnation all had been alcoholic. One of them further dismayed his family by trying to smoke cigarettes when he was scarcely more than a toddler and assured his parents that he had found smoking almost as pleasurable an addiction as drink. Others called for supplies of *bhang* and *charas*, which are drugs popular with lower caste Indians, and declared that they had been very fond of these intoxicants in their former life.

A number of children insisted on acting the role of the profession in which they claimed to have worked. A little Ceylonese girl who recalled the life of a school teacher, dressed up in adult clothes, provided herself with props representing a blackboard and pointer, and spent the day addressing an imaginary class of pupils. It is perhaps not unusual for quite normal children to pretend that they are authoritative figures like teachers, doctors or policemen. Quite extraordinary, however, was the bold young Turkish lad who, purporting to have lived as a nightclub owner, played at dispensing drinks and offered the charms of a female singer. An Indian infant gave her parents cause for concern by demonstrating a complete fearlessness towards snakes and claimed that in her former life she had kept a pet cobra to scare thieves away. And a Burmese girl, Tin Aung Myo, who resolutely maintained that she had once been a Japanese soldier killed in the Burmese jungle during the Second World War, played aggressively boyish military games until she was ten years old. Ever since then – and she is now in her twenties – she has insisted on wearing male clothing and has decided that she is sexually attracted to women rather than men.

Tin Aung Myo has been the subject of a special case report by Dr Stevenson who suggests that trans-sexualist, gender identity problems, which are reported with increasing frequency in the West, could be explained just as well by the reincarnation theory as by the more generally accepted

Freudian hypotheses. He has come across other cases – five of which he has published – in which the child claims to remember a life as a member of the opposite sex in its present existence. In most cases this inclination towards the opposite sex has gradually disappeared as the child grew older, but sometimes, as with Tin Aung Myo, it persists into adulthood.

Inexplicable appetites are not confined to children, of course. Many women when they are pregnant develop bizarre cravings for foods they usually consume in moderation, if at all. A young mother I know was overcome with an unprecedented longing for kippers when she was pregnant and pleaded with her husband to find a fishmonger's shop open at the weekend which could supply her needs. No one seems to have explained this phenomenon very well. In several of Dr Stevenson's cases he has come across something very similar: the pregnant mother has developed a craving – or sometimes a strong dislike – for a certain kind of food. The child has subsequently shown the same craving or dislike which it has put down to an experience from its former life. In other words, Stevenson suggests, even a foetus can show symptoms of previous incarnation and make those symptoms felt in its mother.

Uncanny skills
According to the tenets of modern psychology children have to be taught skills; they are not born with them and do not pick them up spontaneously without having to go through a long learning process. Some of Dr Stevenson's children have inexplicably manifested remarkable skills in infancy, however. An Alaskan boy seemed to have been born with an extensive knowledge of the workings of ships' engines; a Bengali girl had an amazing repertoire of traditional songs and dances she could perform; other children demonstrated advanced skills in such diverse activities as playing the drums, cooking and weaving, and using a sewing machine. The children's explanation was that they had learnt to do these things in their previous life.

Children who reject their parents
In India, where the caste system imposes social barriers much

stronger than even the most entrenched British class prejudice, Dr Stevenson has encountered a number of children who claim to have lived their previous lives as members of superior castes and have therefore berated their parents for their lowly social status. Four Indian boys who remembered earlier lives as upper caste Brahmins developed very snobbish attitudes and demanded special foods and privileges to which, as Brahmins, they thought themselves entitled. Other children who preferred their remembered life to their current one ran away from home in an attempt to find their 'real parents'.

Birthmarks and congenital deformities

An Alaskan boy called Corliss Chotkin Junior claimed to be the reincarnation of his mother's uncle, whose name was Victor Vincent. This claim in no way surprised his mother because Victor Vincent had told her some time before his death that he would be reborn as her next son. So that she would have proof that this state of affairs had truly come to pass, Victor Vincent pointed to two scars he had on his back and on his nose, and told his niece that the boy would have birthmarks on the same spots.

Corliss Chotkin Jr did indeed bear such marks when Dr Stevenson examined him. They were quite unlike normal birthmarks, being three-dimensional and puckered like scars. The doctor managed to get hold of Victor Vincent's hospital records which confirmed that the site, size and shape of one of young Corliss' birthmarks was identical to one of the scars borne by his mother's uncle.

Dr Stevenson has examined some 200 such birthmarks, and in several cases he has been able to gain access to medical records which have shown that the marks corresponded closely with scars or wounds borne by the child's claimed previous personality. Some of the birthmarks are simply areas of increased pigmentation, though usually much larger than the common freckle or brownish birthmark most people have somewhere on their body. Many others, like the ones borne by Corliss Chotkin, are raised and indented and look much more like scars than the usual birthmark. Sometimes the child has a mole which corresponds to a similar mark on the same spot on the body of the individual whose life the child claims to remember.

Children who have been born with deformed limbs or without hands, toes or fingers have recalled gruesome details of their previous lives. The usual explanation the child gives is that it was murdered and mutilated in its previous existence. Other children who have suffered from chronic diseases report that they suffered from the same complaint in their other life. An Indian child, Sukla Gupta, for instance, suffered from facial pimples, Marta Lorenz from bronchitis, Norman Despers from myopia and Bishen Chand Kapoor from an eye complaint. On investigating these cases Dr Stevenson has found that no one else in the child's family suffered from the same complaint, or if they did, it was in a much milder form. He has been able to obtain the medical records of 21 of the individuals whose lives these children claim to remember, and has confirmed that they did indeed have scars or illnesses which corresponded very closely to the children's birthmarks or complaints.

If the child had been born into the same family as its previous personality, one might explain the birthmarks and deformities as a hereditary trait. Corliss Chotkin was after all supposed to be the reincarnation of his uncle. Nevertheless, one would have to stretch genetic theory beyond its present limits to account for most of the startling coincidences Dr Stevenson has reported. And of course if the child claims to remember the life of someone to whom it is completely unrelated, genetics cannot offer an explanation at all.

If we assume that Dr Stevenson is a genuine and scrupulous researcher and has not been the victim of a gigantic hoax played on him by many thousands of people throughout five continents, his observations must be regarded as a truly revolutionary contribution to psychiatry. His insights offer an explanation for several poorly understood conditions.

However, if his theory is a sound one, we are still left with one very big question. Why can't we all remember our past lives? It is a question for which he has only a tentative answer.

Firstly, very nearly all his children began to recall their previous lives at a very early age, almost always when they were between two and six years old, but as they got older the memories grew intermittent and had usually faded altogether by the time they reached their teens or early adulthood. Most came from simple societies where a child is not exposed to the wealth of stimuli which beset infants in modern Western cultures. The glimpses his children got of their former lives were usually partial rather than panoramic, and this faint flicker of recollection would soon be overlaid by the experiences acquired in their new life. Dr Stevenson has also noticed that reincarnated personalities are very often the result of a sudden or violent death in the previous life. In Lebanon and Syria 78 per cent of the lives recalled by children had come to a violent end, in Turkey the figure is 77 per cent, and in most of the other countries he has visited about half the children claim to have died by violence in their previous incarnation.

Among the reincarnated personalities who died natural deaths, two distinct character types emerge – greedy, wealthy men and devout, generous women. Dr Stevenson points out that according to Buddhist beliefs, greedy, wealthy men may remember previous lives because of their attachment to wealth, while the pious women may have 'clarified their minds' through meditation and thereby enhanced and preserved all their memories.

The notion that one's actions in life determine the kind of life one leads after death is common to many religions. But it is, as yet, quite alien to psychiatry. When Dr Stevenson's papers were published in the *Journal of Nervous and Mental Disease*, they were prefaced by very circumspect editorials and commentaries stressing that while the writers found his work intriguing and well-researched, they were not endorsing his theory themselves. One of those commentators suggested: 'Either he is making a colossal mistake, or he will be known . . . as the Galileo of the twentieth century.'

12 Out of the Underground

This book is an outsider's book, not an insider's book. If I had practised any of the therapies described or if I had benefited or suffered from them as a patient, I might have had very different things to say. There are limits to what a journalist can learn from interviews and reading literature. To this extend it is superficial. It is the account of an averagely sceptical and gullible observer with no particular axe to grind.

Scepticism can be a useful instrument and it can also blinker you. If you find it hard to accept that health-restoring energy patterns can be broadcast from a black box, you begin your investigation with a biased mind. You tend to latch on to facts which confirm your disbelief more easily than those which call it into question. And your opinion is more readily swayed by people who present cogent arguments than those who stumble and stammer or who are just plain boring.

In the chapter on Philippino healers I described objects which were supposedly materialized by the psychic surgeon. When native patients were being treated the objects tended to be corncobs, rusty nails and other things which could have been hexed to cause the patient's disease. When Americans and Germans came to be treated the psychic surgeons found that such things were regarded with alarm by the Westerners who associated surgery with blood and gore. The healers promptly began to make blood and gore appear instead. We expect our doctors to go through certain rituals, and if our expectations are not fulfilled we are less inclined to feel better.

Time and again unorthodox practitioners have told me that they get patients 'whose GP had no time for them'.

Could it be that doctors have forgotten the art of ritual? Perhaps we shall find that the wicked drugs people are worried about are not really the cause of iatrogenic disease, but that the doctor does not know how to present the medicine to the patient. I know one GP who cups his hands round bottles and pills before he gives them to the patient to add 'a little bit of healing energy'. Conversely, why not try putting them in the middle of a magic circle and chanting a few words to banish unwanted side-effects? Well, why not? Has anyone tried it?

By concentrating on individual therapies one can forget that most alternative medicine is holistic. It regards man as more than the sum of his parts. Acupuncture, for instance, is itself only one part of Chinese medicine which includes diet, herbs and spiritual welfare. (For the Chinese the idea of a Doctor of Acupuncture would be as absurd as an Englishman styling himself Doctor of Aspirin.) Conventional medics mock fringe practitioners for claiming that they can cure everything. In fact that is not usually their claim. They say they try to cure people, not diseases.

Holistic medicine is not totally ignored by orthodoxy. The ideas of psychiatrist Michael Balint are becoming quite popular with GPs. Dr Balint's belief was that 'by far the most frequently used drug in general practice was the doctor himself. It was not only the bottle of medicine or the box of pills that mattered, but the way the doctor gave them to the patient – in fact the whole atmosphere in which the drug was given and taken.'

Unfortunately, Balint pointed out, 'no guidance whatever is contained in any textbook as to the dosage in which the doctor should prescribe himself, in what form, how frequently nor what his curative and maintenance doses should be.'

Such things are intangible and very difficult to measure objectively. Indeed the standard defence offered by serious practitioners of many holistic therapies when they are told that they should justify their claims by submitting their methods to clinical trials is that many of the benefits they offer their patients cannot be assessed in the impersonal atmosphere of a hospital or research establishment.

This argument plays them straight into the hands of their

critics who retort quite justifiably that no one should expect to be taken seriously as a therapist unless he can prove that his therapy works, and prove it not just to himself but to an impartial observer. The reason why homoeopathy has been regarded as undesirable even by unprejudiced doctors is that homoeopaths have not until recently been prepared to submit their work to the same kind of scrutiny expected of drug therapies. The trials conducted by Dr Gibson and Dr MacNeill, reported in Chapter Three, have shown that the unorthodox can meet orthodoxy on its own ground and acquit itself well. If the homoeopaths can make a serious attempt at winning academic respect, there is absolutely no reason why practitioners of the other 'alternatives' should not do the same.

If the unorthodox are prepared to submit themselves for examination, the medical establishment should be prepared to withdraw their prejudices. Dr Alec Forbes suggested to his colleagues that he should be allowed to set up clinical trials of radionics and the homoeopathic preparation Vita Florum. He was smartly told that such pursuits would be 'unethical'. This attitude is perhaps as dangerous in its way as charlatanry.

There is of course a deep philosophical divide between most scientists and doctors, whose approach is that of the scientific materialist, and the more intelligent fringe practitioners, whose holistic philosophies tend to draw from the mystical traditions of the Orient, where mind is thought to be the creator of matter. Extra-sensory phenomena and reincarnation stick in the materialist's gullet; they do not fit his world view. They are easily swallowed by a holist, however, who sees mind or consciousness as something universal and certainly not restricted to the few cubic inches of grey and pink matter enclosed within the skull.

People can believe what they like, and many of them do. But for a sick person the doctor's beliefs are less important than his ability to help them get well. Britain's legal system is tolerant of the unorthodox and places few restrictions on anyone who wants to practise his or her style of medicine. Alternative medicine is booming, having capitalized on the well-publicized failings of the orthodox medical system. And in an era when all forms of orthodoxy are widely mistrusted, anything which styles itself 'alternative' will *per se* attract supporters. In medicine, however, there should be no alternatives. Curing the sick should not be a sectarian activity. Those who think they have something genuine to offer should be encouraged to prove their worth – or their uselessness. The National Health Service is supposed to be comprehensive, but if hundreds of thousands of patients are being treated privately by unqualified people for complaints which doctors have failed to relieve, the NHS is obviously failing in its function. The alternative therapies should be investigated by independent assessors and if they are found to work they should be made available under the NHS.

Obviously there would be political problems. Doctors would not care for an influx of therapists with motley qualifications, and many of the therapists, who have enjoyed complete clinical freedom in private practice, would not relish being told what was what by an uppish doctor. The whole thing could be brought about with minimal interference to the status quo. if doctors were simply allowed to refer patients to licensed practitioners of approved therapies. As doctors tend to have a wider and deeper knowledge of medicine than the alternative practitioner, it would be wise to insist that if the patient wanted free treatment he should first go to a GP for a diagnosis, rather than go first to the therapist who might vigorously apply treatments which were not relevant to the patient's ills.

All this would require more knowledge on the part of doctors, who would be expected to learn a little about the approved alternatives. And it would require more frankness from the therapists, who would have to justify their claims. Indeed it would require a little more understanding all round.

INDEX